# Writing Spirit

BOOKS BY LYNN V. ANDREWS

*Medicine Woman*

*Spirit Woman*

*Jaguar Woman*

*The Woman of Wyrrd*

*Dark Sister*

*Love and Power*

*Tree of Dreams*

*The Power Deck*

*Teachings Around the Sacred Wheel*

*Writing Spirit*

LYNN V. ANDREWS

# Writing Spirit

Finding Your Creative Soul

JEREMY P. TARCHER / PENGUIN

a member of

Penguin Group (USA) Inc.

JEREMY P. TARCHER/PENGUIN
Published by the Penguin Group
Penguin Group (USA) Inc., 375 Hudson Street, New York, New York 10014, USA ◦
Penguin Group (Canada), 90 Eglinton Avenue East, Suite 700, Toronto, Ontario
M4P 2Y3, Canada (a division of Pearson Penguin Canada Inc.) ◦ Penguin Books Ltd,
80 Strand, London WC2R 0RL, England ◦ Penguin Ireland, 25 St Stephen's Green, Dublin 2,
Ireland (a division of Penguin Books Ltd) ◦ Penguin Group (Australia), 250 Camberwell
Road, Camberwell, Victoria 3124, Australia (a division of Pearson Australia Group Pty Ltd) ◦
Penguin Books India Pvt Ltd, 11 Community Centre, Panchsheel Park, New Delhi–110 017,
India ◦ Penguin Group (NZ), 67 Apollo Drive, Mairangi Bay, Auckland 1311,
New Zealand (a division of Pearson New Zealand Ltd) ◦ Penguin Books (South Africa)
(Pty) Ltd, 24 Sturdee Avenue, Rosebank, Johannesburg 2196, South Africa

Penguin Books Ltd, Registered Offices: 80 Strand, London WC2R 0RL, England

A list of credits and permissions appears on page 238.

The Library of Congress catalogued the hardcover edition as follows:

Andrews, Lynn V.
Writing spirit / Lynn Andrews.
p.    cm.
ISBN 978-1-58542-473-3 (1-58542-473-0)
1. Spiritual life.    2. Creative ability—Religious aspects.
3. Creations (Literary, artistic, etc.)    I. Title.
BL624.A535    2006            2005053884
299'.93—dc22

ISBN 978-1-58542-580-8 (1-58542-580-X; paperback edition)

*Book design by Meighan Cavanaugh*

146119709

## Last Chance Range

The saxophone        plays muted jazz
and I stare out imagining
music as lightning      piercing

the dank sky of the mind
        and where the earth is wet
and shallow        a lotus appears

when I approach the empty page
I think to myself      saxophone
lightning        a lotus

approach        and the poem opens

    wilderness arrives

JACK CRIMMINS

# Contents

# Acknowledgments

I placed the first draft of this book in my agent Al Lowman's hands and went to the ocean. When I returned, tears of happiness were streaming down his face.

"This is so wonderful, Lynn, I will edit it myself. I want this to be my last gift to you." Al was speaking from his hospice bed, and we both knew he didn't have long. I am so grateful for his wild presence in my life.

And so we began our last of eighteen books together. Sitting in a shack by the Santa Barbara sea, we drank his favorite Grey Goose vodka and wept, laughed, edited, as I wrote. Al would take a turn for the worse and be back in the hospice. I would fly home and with the caring and intrepid abilities of Clariss Ritter, who helped edit and decipher the handwritten scribbles of us both, we finished a final draft of this book. Now as I work through Keri English's fine editing from Penguin Books, I hear Al's laughter. I remember the ocean tide coming in on those long afternoons, bringing the scent of salt and new beginnings. I knew the tide of life was receding from Al, drawing him back into a great ocean of consciousness. As we sent this book to my

*Acknowledgments*

visionary publisher, Joel Fotinos, Al passed away on a beautiful sunny morning, in his sleep as he had wished.

So all of you, my muses, surround me in spirit and tell me why I am here without you. This writing acknowledgment is for all the named and nameless beings who have given me so much love, inspiration, and courage in my life. Special thanks to Kathy Duckworth for her unending support of my work.

# Writing Spirit

# Introduction

I flew into Katmandu, Nepal, coming from Hong Kong. I was exhausted. I don't travel well, and jet lag always gets me. I came in the afternoon, over the rolling hills of Nepal and the Himalayas, snow-capped and austere. I was so excited to be in this country and to see Ani, the Nepalese hill woman who is a member of the Sisterhood of the Shields, who are my teachers. We had met only briefly and she had asked me to come. She had said, "I want to teach you about the ways of windhorse, which is the final state of work, of experience before you move into a state of enlightenment."

I got off the plane with many young men who had trekking gear, who were exhausted and needed sleep as badly as I did. When I walked into the airport, my eyes opened wide. I was unprepared for the sights, smells, and the cacophony of sounds emanating from the streets. When you see pictures of Nepal, you don't think of noises and smells and heat. The cab drivers in Nepal never stop honking their horns. Cows wander through the streets. I could look out the doors of the airport and see the sacred cows of the Hindu walking across the street outside.

As I turned to get my luggage, I saw an old woman standing in a corner in the shadows of the airport. There was so much noise and so many different kinds of people. There was a strangeness and an excitement in the atmosphere, like being on the edge of war, which unbeknownst to me at that time was true. I couldn't take my eyes off the woman standing in the corner. She was thin, tall, and draped in turquoise and ancient silver and pieces of coral. She wore several different fabrics overlapping one another, giving her the look of tradition and a quality of timelessness and beauty. Her eyes glittered like the silver that hung all the way to her waist. Her face was like ancient bark on a tree, lined and crevassed with age and humor. Her hair was long and tied back. It was a cool morning, and she had a turquoise-colored pashmina shawl draped over her shoulders. She stood so still that cobwebs could have grown between the wall and her and never be broken. She watched me. Her face didn't change, but her eyes very slightly lit up. I thought maybe she was waiting for me, but she made no move toward me except with her spirit. I felt cocooned by her intent. I had been very tired. Now there were surges of energy moving through my belly. I was so excited.

I picked up my bags, and as I started to walk toward the front door with the sound and the dust and the racket outside, I felt the old woman's eyes on my back. I moved to the side as the trekkers rushed by me. Then I turned, and the woman walked toward me. It was not Ani but a woman who was in her own way beyond compare, a shaman woman of the mountains, of the Himalayas, of the valleys. I could feel the rhododendrons and fuchsia beautiful within her. I could hear the wind when I looked into her eyes.

## Introduction

She placed her hand on my arm. Her hand, like those of most of the women in the Sisterhood, was brown and weathered and very strong. She searched my face for a moment as if looking for something. It intimidated me, and she nodded, seeing that inside me. She wanted me to feel comfortable and safe.

Your sacred space is where you can find yourself again and again.
— JOSEPH CAMPBELL

# CLOSED DOORS
# AND APPLE TREES

In the beginning the doors would close to my soul, to my feelings, to my heart. I was about five years old and would climb up into the apple trees. There I would write to open those doors again. I never wanted to live without those doors being open, even though it made me more sensitive, more vulnerable and open to pain. Writing in the apple trees was wonderful. The trees brought me closer to the sky, closer to the stars. I remembered those apple trees when Agnes said to me years later, "We are made from stars and to the stars we must one day return." I knew what it felt like to be a star, to follow slowly through the universe, shining down on the earth. I would go out of my body. I wanted to get away from the hurt and the depression of my unsettled family. So in my imagination I would go to the heavens and become a star. I would become its light.

One apple tree in particular, an old grandmother tree, was my favorite. I would climb up in her. There was a fork in her branches and those branches would hold me. I could lean back a little into the crook of her arms. I could even reach up and pick an apple, and it would make her happy that I would share in her flavor, the juice of life that she so graciously shared with me. I dug trenches, fertilized and watered the orchard. I became part of her and she became part of me. As I ate those apples, I would begin to write about how good that made me feel. I would write about Spice and Spunk, two little pinto ponies. My dad always made sure that I had a horse and a dog. Those animals helped me to stay grounded, helped me to find my joy early on. At five and six years old, I would climb down from the apple tree with my apples and my writing. Then I would go out to my horse and give her an apple, letting her feel the comfort of the old grandmother tree. She would chew and nicker softly in my ear. She, too, felt the joy. Standing on a bale of hay, I would lift up a saddle with a blanket under it and place it on her back. I would bridle her, and leaving my notebook in the barn I would get on her and ride out toward the wilderness. My father would always call after me, "Be back by sunset." I am amazed when I look back at that and how young I really was. His trust in me made me feel powerful. He knew that I would be home by sunset, and I always was.

I rode all day in the wilderness and would come across bears and snakes and badgers. My best friend in grade school, Beverly, a Native American girl, would get on her horse and ride with me down the road and out toward Dead Man's Creek. We would take our horses across the plains. We would play games and pretend that we were the stars again, chasing each other across the universe. I knew how to be a star, to feel that light. From then on, as I wrote stories about my horses and dogs—but not much about people— I learned to search for the light that had fallen to the earth. I would pick up that shine with my pencil and paper and in some way try to re-create that beautiful light from the stars so that I could share it and illumine others with it. My intent through my writing was always to bring the flavor of those apples, the comfort of grandmother tree, the joy I felt when I touched the coolness of her bark, and the feel of the wind in my hair as I galloped across the meadows, experiencing the mystery of the wilderness.

I was always climbing in trees. Once we were pulling a trailer across the country from Massachusetts to Washington. Toward dark one evening I crawled up in a tree and a man came to my father and asked, "What is that old man doing up in that tree?"

Dad said, "What are you talking about?"

"Come, over here," the man said.

I called down and my voice was very low, like a man's voice. That was the first time that I became aware that I had an odd voice. My mother had me study voice and speaking early on in my grade school years so I could learn to lift my voice up a little, because it was "too low."

Sitting on the porch one morning over coffee and tea, I told Agnes and Ruby this story. Agnes looked at me in her usual skeptical and funny way and said, "Well, it sounds to me like you were a George boy."

I said, laughing, "Agnes, what are you talking about? What is a George boy?"

"Oh, you know, when girls act like boys."

I burst out laughing and said, "You mean tomboy."

She said, "Oh, yeah, I knew that—tomboy."

Trees were the tree of life to me. They protected me. I could physically lift up above things the way I did in my spirit. I would go up in the trees and talk to God. I never saw God in a form but as an experience, as the essence of my soul. When I was sad, which was most of the time, I would climb up in the grandmother tree and talk to her. Then I would talk to God. Early on I asked if I could go to a Catholic school, because I knew that they had chapels where you could pray. My dad took me to Holy Name School in Spokane. There I learned to play the piano. It was about then that I stopped climbing in trees, because everybody thought it was extremely peculiar for this little girl in a uniform to be way up high in a tree. But I still remembered the grandmother tree and the fruits that she gave me in so many ways.

The trees are sacred to me. The groves grow in circles, and you can sit in the middle of that circle and do ceremony with the stars. I always had a sense of the tree of life and all that means. I would think of the branches of the tree as aspects of my family and the trunk of the tree as being like God and the life force that is a current through us all.

I could never be myself as a child. I had to be careful. As a result of that, I would become sad or depressed, so I would play in the orchard. Because the apples would sometimes fall on my head, I would say, "The apples are falling from the sky." Many years later, after my father had passed away and I had not seen him for years because I was very afraid of him, for the first time I went to where he lived, and on his wall he had made a painting of apples falling from the sky. I have that painting to this day.

I think when you cannot be yourself, it makes you want to write, because in your writing, you can be who you truly are. You can write characters that sometimes can live out the dreams that you are afraid to speak of, and that's a good thing. I think that is when writing really makes you feel better. So often, I talk to writers who agonize through every page. They hate their writing; they hate to write. They don't like the process, but they are possessed by the muse. So that is what they do. They cannot do otherwise.

I have always been quizzical about this, because I have always loved to be free.

I am a writer who is not trying to be a good writer, not trying to write for money or fame or rewards. I began writing as a very young girl climbing up in an apple tree, wanting to feel better. I love books. I love paper. I love the craft of putting a book together. I love publishing. I love the skill of words being strung together in an artful, inspiring way. I don't look at a novel or a book or a piece of writing for syntax or grammar. I look at it to change me somehow, to move me beyond myself, to entertain me in some way. I read to learn something. I read what teaches me. This can all be done in the way a book is written.

When I consider writing a book about writing, I have to laugh because I am not writing about writing: I am writing about the soul. I am not a religious person; I am a spiritual person. I want to have my dialogue with the divine. Maybe that means a tree or a rock or a magnificent being of light that I cannot explain. To me writing is a dream. It is a symbol. It is the use of the appropriate word for the feeling, the emotion, the event that I am trying to portray. Certainly, I have been known as a spiritual writer; I have written eighteen books that have been published by wonderful publishers.

My sense of writing has been to explore the unknown mystery of life. To me, that mystery is a harmony, a construct of energy forms made out of light, electricity, life-forms that defy the imagination or description because they are animated by a source beyond words or explanation. It is that source that I have always been in search of. I might find that source in a book on the wisdom of ancient Egypt, such as *The Secret Teachings* by Gene Kieffer, or the look of a mountain at sunrise or sunset, the central darkness of the sun even though it is surrounded by radiance: the creative force of life. I am incredibly impatient with verbal wanderings that border on masturbation of the spirit, emoting, and the love of the author for the sound of his own voice.

Hemingway had a magnificent ability to write the essence of things, the simplicity, taking out all the extraneous words that bled off the energy of what he was saying. Anaïs Nin wrote about her emotions. It was not that her emotions were so fascinating, it was the way she described them. Her talent and ability are almost beyond compare. In her early days in Paris with Laurence Durrell and Henry Miller, none of them could get published because of what they were writing about. Publishers would say to Anaïs, "Why are you writing about your emotions? That doesn't have any interest to people." Yet Anaïs became one of the most treasured writers of her time, as did the other two. What the publishers of that era didn't understand is that people, readers, want to identify with what you write. They want to come from the heart and the soul; they want to read books that come from the soul. They want to grow, often in spite of themselves. They want to be entertained, yes, but in a way that speaks to them from the heart.

To me, entertainment is moving into the unknown, the uncharted areas, the landscape of the mysteries of mind, emotion, spirit, and magic. The shadow has a great deal to do with that, the shadow self. Shadow defines the light, and yet shadow can become so overwhelming that you don't see the light anymore.

Shakespeare is one of the great writers of the shadow, one of the great "tragedy-makers" of all time. He wrote about the force of nature and experiences upon the mind and the soul. He outlined so magnificently the wildness of emotions that overtakes the mind, judgment that becomes subject to an inner calling that oftentimes challenges our understanding. He had a way of placing words so that power and strength and agony and joy were all created in a sentence. For instance, in *Macbeth* he writes, "What are these / So wither'd and so wild in their attire, / That look not like the inhabitants o' the earth / And yet are on't?" He infuses his environment with action and desperation, reaction, and dreadful, marvelous truth. His reader's field of awareness is then prepared for all that follows.

*Macbeth* is different in so many ways from Shakespeare's other plays. I always feel as if I'm on the verge of stepping into the abyss: the murder, the intrigue that Lady Macbeth created in her husband, and the horror and haunting quality of the darkness of the soul that finally take Lady Macbeth's life. She takes her own life, but really the haunting takes her, hesitantly, I say, the way a plot or story stalks you until you write it. If you look at a story, a paradigm, or a darkness long enough, it begins to take you. I think perhaps that is a quality of what Shakespeare was illustrating, as when Macbeth resolves to rid himself of Macduff, "That I may tell pale-hearted fear it lies / And sleep in spite of thunder." And Lady Macbeth, so often the baffling solutions to life, the impressions of her lofty dreams and aspirations, and her cries under her own inability to deal with the haunting crimes she is contemplating: "Come, you spirits / That tend on mortal thoughts, unsex me here, / And fill me from the crown to the toe top-full / Of direst cruelty! Make thick my blood; / Stop up the access and passage to remorse, / That no compunctious visitings of nature / Shake my fell purpose, nor keep peace between / The effect and it!" The abyss begins to overtake them all because of a decision made out of greed and without an understanding of the larger vision of life and death (although far be it from me to know the incredible vision and thirst that was within that writer's soul). *Macbeth* is felt deep within the contest between life and death; the decisions that are made at the moment of human compulsion for riches, for superiority, for kingship, for control of all that lives within each of us. The play has a rugged severity that leads us deep into the dark well of human emotions, into the sires of murder, deception, and unholy greed. We feel the "air-drawn dagger" that slices into the fruits of the characters' extraordinary expectations. They are all part of that shadow self that is within us and is so beautifully, beautifully articulated in the plays of William Shakespeare.

I am more interested in the light and the personification of light. In ancient Egypt, Akhenaton built cities of light with no roofs so that the sunlight was always shining down upon the people. Why? I wonder if, perhaps, it is because within the light of the sun, within the light of a radiant being is an illuminated soul and the potential not only for one person's transformation but also for the transformation of all those who touch her. In ancient times it was said by my teachers that sunlight actually redefined and helped birth new and as yet unknown codes of higher consciousness. That is how I approach my process of writing.

I am a mystic. I have studied shamanism for most of my life. Although I am not Catholic, I grew up in Catholic schools and loved all of my teachers, who were nuns and priests. I loved, most of all, the ability to go into the chapel and pray. I have never tried to name the god or goddess. To me, it is a feeling, a sense. I realize that emotion is one thing and feeling is another. Emotion can result in something very chaotic and scattered, with polarities of all kinds, love and anger and hatred. Emotion drives feeling, the feeling of ecstatic joy, the simplicity of the oneness within a paragraph, undefined but known, as with a writer like Neruda or García Lorca. The ever-present sense of death, or *duende,* that some writers have is what I look for, because I understand it. I find it seductive and something I cannot ignore.

## Closed Doors and Apple Trees

The writer's soul is where my passion and curiosity live. It is not how or what you write that is important. It is your creative spirit. The musician, the writer, the artist within the inspirational moment needs to be held in the most precious of ways, not only by the world (which we very seldom are) but, more important, by the writer, the creator, the creative being. When I observe many of the creative people I know in the world, I see that we often deform ourselves to fit into a society that is entertained by us but doesn't know us, doesn't understand us, and therefore is most often leery of us in one way or another. As human beings, we want to be loved, understood, and cared for, and so we will begin to deform our true flow of spirit so that we fit in and become acceptable somehow. We hide, and with that hiding and distortion often come writer's block and the inability to practice what we do, our magic, and become successful at it. Unconsciously we think that if we claim our power, then we will no longer be loved. We think that if we become deified, then maybe we will be crucified. We become careful, like abused children, so that we won't be hit, so that "they" won't really see us. We become the invisible ones.

I write about how we care for ourselves in a world that does not know how to appreciate us and is frightened of us because we imply change. I survive through the shamanistic approach, which is understanding the energies of our bodies and our environment and the universe around us so that we can then choreograph those energies. It is one way to absorb the magic, understand and translate it, and live within the essence of that magic.

Certain shamans and writers talk about erasing personal history. This is not the way of my teachers, nor is it the practice which I follow as a teacher and a healer. For writers, especially, I think that is a dangerous vision. I believe that we have chosen our bodies and our life experiences to teach us things. To erase personal history means to let go not only of the people in your history, and the difficulties and abuse, but also of the lessons of life that these experiences teach you, the *knowing* that comes from your own personal history. It is this knowing, these experiences, that animates your writing, that give it depth, that make it so readable. You can't remember the knowing without remembering the circumstances. Better than the erasing of personal history is to go into the middle of your experience as it is and as you are resolving it *and write about it*. Let it become your characters. Let all of that experience be part of your gift to people. That's what enables you to be humble in the face of any corruption or difficulty. It allows you the understanding and depth of character that is so needed to write the truth of any individual in your stories.

I love and treasure life experience. Life can be painful. It often takes a tremendous amount of energy to get from one end of a day to the other, and difficult times can bleed off a tremendous amount of our power while we are going through them. But always we find, after we have weathered our difficulties, that they have brought us so much personal growth and understanding. It is not possible to eliminate all of the things that bleed off our power as we go through life. But in learning from and growing through them, we can create great personal power in our lives, and this, in turn, can become the source of great writing.

Whatever you see as your personal reality, your power within yourself becomes the source of your writing. I would definitely encourage you to look at how you unnecessarily bleed away your energy every day. If you bleed away your power through negativity, through judgment, argument, uncontrolled anger, through relationships that are not kind and useful to you, that are dysfunctional in some way, then you are doing a great disservice to your writing process as well as to your life. We certainly don't want to

live in our addiction to pain and our addiction to fear and to confusion, which so many writers end up doing. We came here to
evolve out of our addictions to the physical realm. Then we can
partake of the physical realm with joy, and it brings us joy. The
experience of life and personal history is the basis of many aspects
of joy, and that is what we came here to learn. It contains the mirrors that are created by the physical realm, by your desire, your
contentment, by your feelings driven by your emotions and all of
what you are. Through your efforts to love and make choices, you
discover the meaning of your personal history. Your personal history should be cherished, not discarded. I will have savored every
moment of this life and experienced the depths of the joy and the
depths of the pain and the humor that are elicited from all of the
reflections I create. I will live with that joy. I will write that joy
and how it came to be.

You are the whole Ocean. Why send out for a sip of dew?    —RUMI

# HEROES

I feel that everyone is a hero in his or her own life. My approach to writing is influenced by that view. In all of my books, with the exception of my workbooks, I have related my experiences through that lens. So, who are you as hero? If this seems difficult to relate to, then play with this concept and see how your attitude shifts. Explore the many profound books by Joseph Campbell.

I like to explore Joseph Campbell's stages of the hero's journey in *The Power of Myth* as they apply to my own work. I wrote *Medicine Woman* long before his book was written, but as he says, "All stories consist of a few common structural elements found universally in myths, fairy tales, dreams and movies. They are known collectively as the hero's journey. Understanding these elements and their use in modern writing is the object of our quest. Used wisely, these ancient tools of the storytellers' craft still have tremendous power to heal our people and make the world a better place."

Before I ever write about my experiences, I choreograph my

plot and ideas through ancient myths like Persephone, the Greek goddess who dives deep into her own darkness, or Spider Woman, the Dineh (Navajo) deity who wove up the reality of our world with luminous fibers like those of a spider's web reflecting the light of the moon. I don't take the myth into my writing; rather, I surround my story with the fragrance of ancient times and wisdom. It's as if I take each word I have written and wash it with the profound depths of the sacred pond reflected, for example, in Norse or Celtic mythology. Ancient myths have so much to teach us about ourselves and the deeper meaning of life.

To be able to teach anything or even to learn, the beginning has to exist for you. What is your origin? Where are your people from? If you don't know who your ancestors were, then it would be fascinating to become what you dream of and create your own personal mythology. If you don't know your family origin, create it; create the stories and events that helped to shape your grandparents, and their ancestors before them. Write your own personal myth, or at least an outline of it, and then compare the story you are writing to your own personal myth. In what ways are you a hero in your own life? What are the myths to which you relate most strongly, and how do they influence you and your writing?

Not to dream more boldly may turn out to be, in view of present realities, simply irresponsible.  —George Leonard

# CLIMB YOUR
# TREE OF DREAMS

*"In the Tree of Dreams there is a song," Face in the Water said as we sat together in ceremony in the Sonoran Desert of Arizona. "Like any other living thing, it has a song to be sung. To lose your song is to lose your soul. The song in the tree is something to be listened for very, very carefully. It teaches you that life is never ending."*

*Smoke from the fire whirled around us in purple-gray plumes, creating mysterious shadows in the air.*

*"As the leaves begin to drop from the tree in autumn," she continued, "a harmonic is created. The harmonic is different with every leaf that falls and different again for every tree. The Tree of Dreams is you and me. We are all a tree of dreams. We are filled with yearning and joy and love. We are filled with the teachings that we have received and the experiences that we have had. Our branches are the different times of our lives. The leaves are the experiences—the colors, textures, the aspects of the divine. As the leaves fall, the song*

*can be heard, a new song that plays on the wind and is communicated to other trees, if they are listening.*

*"The whale people who live in the North speak about the great whale and how, when she sings a song, it is heard sometimes a thousand miles away. Another whale picks up that song, and the echo is heard another thousand miles away. This goes on until the song is created around the world by all whales singing in unison.*

*"The music that forms the dropping of the leaves is similar. The song that was very much your own blends to create a harmony with other songs as it touches the earth. It is at that moment that all leaves become one, surrounding the earth with crimson, orange, red, and gold. . . .*

*"You have your song. You have learned about the ways of power early in your work with us. As long as you have your song, you can never lose your direction or your vision. Remember, the Owl will take you to your Tree of Dreams. You're not done here yet. The tree holds the other dreamers who are waiting to help you. Don't stray off the track—you know that. Follow your song line. It connects you to what is good and powerful for you. You live in both worlds. You live in spirit and you live on the earth. This is not an easy song to sing, but teaching the young ones to treasure their elderhood is the finest gift you can give, and you will do it well. As the leaves are falling, the new ones begin to grow. That is law. That is your story work. One of the joys of elderhood is telling your story. This is our power before we die. We can pass on what we have learned. Our legacy is thousands of years old. Let it flow through your lips. Anyone can take up the drum and talk to the Great Spirit and join you in a chant. It has always been that way. Your work here for the old ones is just beginning. I am here for you."★*

---

★Lynn Andrews, *Tree of Dreams* (New York: Tarcher/Putnam, 2001).

Imagine that you as a writer are a wise elder looking back on your life, reflecting on your legacy. If you were to write your legacy, what would you say? What would your story be? What would you like those who come after you to know of your experience? What do you wish your legacy to be in this life?

In *Windhorse Woman* I wrote of my work with the Sacred Book of the Child. This is a book that was seeded here, so I was told by the women of the Sisterhood of the Shields, in a remote valley in Tibet by the great beings from the stars in ancient times. As Agnes Whistling Elk says, *"We are made from stars, and to the stars we must one day return."* The Sacred Book of the Child is an Akashic record of a kind, a sacred text that outlines your lifetime from the beginning to the end of time, your past and future lives, everything. You open the book of your history and everything that you are here to learn in your lifetime is there, what you are moving toward, what it is that you are trying to manifest along your path of heart and writing in the process of enlightenment. You can find it now.

Close your eyes and dream. There is a cave within the earth which you have visited many times, whether you realize this on a conscious level or not. Visit it now on a conscious level. Return to the cave within the earth where you first encountered the Sacred Book of the Child, even though you didn't know that was what it was at the time. Place your hands on its cover. Feel its leather binding, very old, ancient leather with gold lettering on it. Touch once again the Sacred Book of the Child. Trace the raised lettering with your fingers and open the book with great care and intent. As you open the book to a blank page, pick up the beautiful gold fountain pen that lies beside it.

When we write, we separate. Writing is a lonely pursuit, and as a result we sometimes see reality as compartmentalized when in truth there is a oneness between you and all people who are creators. Sadly we don't always have a chance to experience that oneness or exchange ideas. Nature is what heals that feeling of separateness. Imagine now that you are a part of nature, you are a part of the oneness. You are a tree.

Imagine that you are a great tree. You are a tree of dreams. Perhaps you are an ancient oak surrounded by your family of oaks and maples and all the great trees of the forest. Perhaps you are a great pine tree like a cedar, deeply rooted into the body of a steep mountain that overlooks a valley and a river flowing far below you. Visualize the kind of tree that you are. See yourself as this great tree, deeply rooted in the earth, solid and strong within your trunk with great branches like arms reaching up to the sky. Feel the wind in your branches, bringing voice and laughter to your leaves or pine needles. Feel the air currents surrounding you and the sunlight pouring down from the heavens, filling you with energy and power. Move your roots deep now into Mother Earth, feeling the coolness, the dark womb that nourishes you so well.

You are a Tree of Dreams and your act of power lives within the very fibers and cells and beingness of this tree that you are. Your act of power has a cycle that is similar to a great tree. Your act of power moves through the seasons of existence, the budding, the blooming, the falling of your leaves or your needles, the shedding and sharing of your manifestations with the world, and then you rest within the wintering of your dreams and realization. Describe yourself as a tree. How does this tree relate to your writing?

You are a writer. Your act of power is the book or the story that you are creating. That is what is written for you in the Sacred Book of the Child. It is time now for you to bloom.

One does not impose one's will on a space. One listens.

—Louis Kahn

# DISCIPLESHIP

Discipleship as described by the Rosicrucians and by Agnes Whistling Elk, my shaman teacher from the north of Canada, is actually similar to any discipline of higher consciousness, I believe. In a sense a writer is in an apprenticeship to power, just as an initiate in the Himalayas is in an apprenticeship. There are stages or levels that you approach, that I will define to help you see yourself from a new perspective.

In my book *Windhorse Woman*, Ani, a Nepalese hill woman, was working with me. We were in an old sod village in the foothills of the Annapurna. The village was like an Indian pueblo of the American Southwest. Children played outside along a sparkling creek, and ravens landed along the rim of the low buildings, calling out messages to one another. Ani, her face strong and weathered by the mountain winds, was smiling at my fidgeting. I have always found it bothersome to sit on the ground in the lotus position for hours on end. The room was darker inside and the candlelight glimmered, reflecting the pieces of mica in the walls.

> *"Your searching has become like a meditation,"* Ani said to me. *"You, like anyone, cannot ask a question beyond your level. It is a law of nature. Your meditation, your being becomes elevated through your searching. I cannot stand in the way of that. You cannot manipulate the laws of nature beyond your level. People who have grasped higher laws are only people who have reached a level where they won't misuse that knowledge. Your Einstein searched and searched for truth, and finally it came to him. If he would have mis-used that wisdom he could not have conceived of it. All great scientists agree on that. What lesser people do with that knowledge is something else. No one who has abilities and has grasped higher laws could ever hurt anyone."**

You are entering a new path as a writer. As Ani would say, "You are answering the call." Who is calling you to write? Where does writing live inside you? You might want to take a few minutes to think about this; scan your body if you will and jot down what you find. It could be very important.

There are tests for a writer. The test that comes next is a process of discovering unrealized powers and talents within you. You recognize a need in the world for a unique voice that is your own. But how do you find that voice? First of all, you become more intimate with yourself by writing about your feelings and relationships. I would urge you to do this now.

---

*Lynn Andrews, *Windhorse Woman* (New York: Warner Books, 1989).

Many writers form writers' block of one kind or another. You ask for the highest good and are suddenly confronted in some way by that goal, and you are stopped in your advancement. Some writers will stand their ground and go deeper, but others will cry and ask for the demands of their craft to go away. You are looking at a revolution in your life, and either you run away or you move to master it. "You cannot gain the greater things in life on the same terms as the lesser." You cannot make affirmations about how great you are and receive the same epiphanies that will come with meditating on an ancient tanka. In meditation, you begin to know strength. In testing that strength with your mind and heart, you begin to know what kind of strength you have.

*Art does not come from thinking, but from responding.*

— CORITA KENT

# YOUR WRITING
# POWER ANIMAL

I assume you write because as a writer you can't not write. You have a passion that is rare and you want to take action, you want to write. So write! Write without hesitation. Write without thinking in the first instance about your writing. If you think about your writing, it can stifle your creativity.

There is a similarity here to brush painting on paper. Once the brush is touched to the paper, the stroke can never be reformed. The paper is so absorbent. The painter must apply her brush without hesitation, without rethinking and thinking about the outcome. A Zen master says, "When you eat, eat; when you sleep, sleep." Once you have a concept that is complete, let it become part of you. When a painter picks up a brush and paints, it becomes an extension of his intent. The dream in his heart becomes one with the canvas. He may not even be completely conscious of his movements. Thought has moved into the mastery of color, form, and the divine impulse that drives him.

Once Fritz Scholder did a painting of me. Fritz was an American artist of Native American and German descent and a renaissance man of his time. He was a writer who created magnificent paintings, lithographs, monotypes, and sculptures of his impressions of life. He lived in New Mexico and Arizona until the end of his life in 2005, and he was a mentor to me and a dear, dear friend for more than thirty years. He taught me some invaluable things about the balance of light and color and particularly balance between my artist self and my business self. An aspect of this book is dedicated to Fritz and to my good friend Hunter S. Thompson, who also died in 2005.

At the time that Fritz painted me, we sat together for a time in his Arizona studio listening to the water fountain and the birds in the Palo Verde trees. My large wooden armchair was covered with spatters of oil paint in reds, blues, and yellows. Fritz sat on a rickety stool, then rose and paced about. He turned his back to me, paintbrush in hand, and began to splash color with great power and abandon all over the large canvas. Not once did he observe me or talk. For all intents and purposes he was lost in his dream of who he felt I was. It was exciting, stimulating, and fascinating. Over two hours had sped by when suddenly he swiveled around and stared at me with overcast eyes and asked, "What have I done? What did I do?" He held his brush in front of him still dripping with yellow ochre. He was no more aware of what he was painting than I was of breathing.

If you think about your writing or your art while you are creating it, then your work is no longer spontaneous. If an archer thinks about his arrow as he pulls back the bow, he will never hit his mark. You want to write about the moon, not the moon's reflection. Have no second thoughts when you play golf, when you paint, or when you write a sentence. Later, much later, you may want to edit. That is impossible with brushstroke on paper, and I mention Zen painting because this art is a wonderful study for any writer. Why? Because thinking about what you write and the outcome and the acceptance of the outcome can be a disease that could keep you from ever producing the wondrous mysteries of creativity that live inside you. How many times as a writer have you thrashed around, sleepless and exhausted, trying to transform your throbbing ideas into words on paper? You're full of fear and desire for success. Take some watercolors and paint in spontaneous brushstrokes the feeling, intent, *and* mystery of what you are writing. What do the strokes, colors, intensity mean?

Twin Dreamers, a powerful Kuna Indian shaman woman, prowled around me like a panther one night while we were sitting at a campfire in the foothills of the Cascade Mountains. Then she stopped without warning and pinned me with her blazing eyes and said, "You're fidgeting, little one."

I nodded in agreement.

"Don't you know that a story is stalking you?"

"What do you mean?" I asked.

"A story once it finds its teller will stalk you endlessly, like a wolf stalks a caribou. A wolf will follow his prey for weeks, biting from time to time at its heels. Each nip leaves a small trail of blood. In your case, your essence, the wolf, the story, can always find you and you alone. You are being nipped, Black Wolf [the name they had given me]. It is your destiny. As a caribou is transformed from life-giving food back into spirit, so are you transformed as a storyteller. You in a sense become transformed by the powerful energy of a story. You don't transform back into spirit, but you become critically aware of the force of creative spirit within you. You become eaten by this story, and your readers in turn. They eat of your essence and empower themselves with food for their souls, and you as a creator become empowered by the process."

I stared at Twin Dreamers, realizing deep inside myself the truth of her words. When I begin to prepare a writing project, I find myself circling for days through my house, setting all my furniture, clothes, kitchen items, and my office in order. Partly, I'm distracting myself from what I need to do. But, mostly, I'm aware of what my Native teachers have taught me about my original nature, what we call a symbolic animal self. I circle my habitat like a wolf, taking in experience and storing it like food for the winter. Finally I settle down and arrange all my research and materials. I begin to put words on paper.

Sometimes I find it helpful in the creative process to see myself and others in a different perspective from the usual. See yourself as an animal. Describe your animal self. As I have worked with students around the world, I find that helping them discover another side or aspect of themselves helps free their creative boundaries and allows them to soar into new dimensions in their work. Certainly I have found this for myself as well. In my book *Medicine Woman,* I wrote of my experience with Agnes Whistling Elk and my power animal nature:

> Agnes dished me up a bowl of hot soup with a strange, rich taste. The dusk was circling round us in gray shadows, encroaching upon the small flickering light of our candle. A soft wind blew through the open door. Agnes sat on the bed sewing on an old mackinaw. Without looking up at me, she asked, "Lynn, what do you really want?"
>
> "What do you think I want? I want the marriage basket."
>
> Agnes said nothing. I sipped the last drop of soup and put the spoon down. Agnes laid the mackinaw aside and looked at me directly.

*"To get the marriage basket, you must become the proper receptacle," she said. "You must ripen your void so that the energy of what you want, in this case the basket, will flow magnetically toward your belly. You must become what she wants so that there is no separating you. When you think of yourself as a separate entity, you will obstruct that current and the basket will defeat you."*

*I was bewildered by these terms. "How will I know when I have ripened my void?"*

*"You will simply become aware of your power. You will feel your time. You cannot avoid it."*

*"Agnes, I don't understand your terminology. How can I learn all these things?"*

*"That's why you are here, to learn."*

*She put the mackinaw in her dresser drawer, walked out onto the porch and sat down. I poured a cup of tea and followed. Agnes was watching the northern lights. Gold and pink, they seemed to be heralding a carnival on the other side of the world. I sat down on the steps and marveled at the play of color across this strange woman's face. I felt a special tenderness for her. Her face was a messenger of great pain to me because it reminded me that what I had known all my life was dying. I couldn't even explain to myself how I was different, but I knew I was evolving into a person I wouldn't have recognized a few months ago. It was like being in love.*

*"Tonight the grandparents have a vital gift for you. I'm going to give you your medicine." Agnes patted the wooden boards and motioned me to sit closer to her. "If you were an animal, what would you be?"*

*I was puzzled. "You are always asking me questions that I have a hard time answering." I thought for a few minutes and then said, "I've always loved horses, or maybe a deer."*

*Agnes smiled at me. "You are a black wolf."*

*She watched my reaction and then put out a hand and touched my forehead. "Waken within yourself." She took her finger away. The touch gave me a peculiar sensation throughout my body.*

*"You are the black wolf instead of the white wolf because you wear the black cloak of contemplation. If you were the white wolf, you would be more outward, more extroverted. You track through the forests for what you want and then come back to the pack and curl up in the sun and think about it. You're a lone wolf who is afraid of being alone. Let me tell you a story.*

*"In the beginning when the world was formed, the chiefs sent the wolf cubs out to explore and measure the world. They went down all the trails of the world and said, 'This is the way it is and that's the way it was.' Wolf medicine means measure. Wolves are good mathematicians if they want to be. If you are one with your medicine you can never be tricked because you've been down all the trails. It's very powerful and hypnotic medicine.*

*"I'll give you an example. The wolf goes down to the river in the early morning. He sees his breakfast swimming out there and dances playfully along the bank. All the geese are close enough, he jumps into the water and kills as many geese as he needs—his can be a very dangerous medicine. A hunter would be very lucky to kill or trap even one wolf, and that's because the wolf teaches the other wolves what the hunters are up to. And if you were the hunter, it would be impossible. You cannot kill your own medicine. If you did, you'd be in very big trouble.*

*"The wolves set up the first school. They were the first teachers. The wolf lives in a way that makes his pack strong. He always provides food for the aged and sick, trains the pups, and defends his territory against other wolves. He tracks like no other animal. He has stamina, and he can go without food for great periods of time. The*

*wolf is big medicine, and you must remember I didn't choose the wolf for you. You are wolf."*

*Agnes sat back.*

*"I'm beginning to see. You've touched something deep inside me," I said. "I do feel sort of like a wolf. I love to discover new trails, and I feel at the center of my being a new kind of awareness. Storm must have known my medicine, because he gave me a piece of wolf fur. What is the purpose of having medicine?"*

*I leaned back against the post, amazed at how wolf-like I was feeling.*

*"The purpose of medicine is power. You go to a psychiatrist and he tells you your head is fouled up. What he's doing is helping you to introspect and learn about your own character. But since native people have observed the four-leggeds and the winged ones and all the forces of nature for thousands of years, we know your closest kinship. When I tell you you're the black wolf, you look within yourself and you know that you truly are. When you understand the powers of the black wolf, you too will have those powers. All the medicines are good and have power. White people have this thing that says, 'I'm not a snake. I'm not a squirrel. I'm something important.' They separate, and that's their tragedy."*

*For a moment Agnes stared at me, her eyes holding the swiftly moving hues of the northern lights. My mind was filled with this new information. I took the wolf fur out of my pocket and felt its softness. Agnes got up abruptly and we went inside the cabin without saying anything further."*★

---

★Lynn Andrews, *Medicine Woman* (San Francisco: Harper & Row, 1981).

When I identified my "writing power animal," my creative force was changed and I became reborn in a sense. Finally I understood so much more about myself. This has nothing to do with faith, religion, tradition, or race. Your writing power animal is a symbolic description of your inner nature as a creative person. For instance, let's say that there are animal categories for writers. Simply play with this idea for a moment.

1. *Grazers:* Deer, elk, moose, horses, antelope, and all those related beings who graze to survive. People who are themselves grazers are wonderful at research, academics, perusing history, facts, and journalism. They find green pastures and, eating, they reform the information back out. Grazers listen well and adapt quickly. Perfecting your own style can be hard for you.

2. *Predators:* Predators are great hunters that are normally carnivorous. They kill to survive. This is a much more aggressive person, who never stops sniffing the wind for prey, e.g., wolf people hunting to eat and to learn. Wolves are the original teachers who bring back information to the pack and teach it to their young. Cat people, pumas, lions, panthers, hunt to eat and hunt to play. Eagles and hawks watch for a long time and then dive, snatch, and eat later. A predatory writer is insatiable for knowledge, a good story, excitement, often danger, and a good challenge. Predators work off the elements and choose their prey or story carefully. They'll often leave a fight of resistance and go on to the next thing. These writers have great ideas but need to follow them through to the end.

3. *Songbirds:* Songbirds are hunting for seeds. They flit and fly, mate, and create nests or stories. They are more fragile

than grazers and predators. But they are enormously agile. All birds, if they see trouble, simply fly above it and away. Romance writers and storytellers are often songbirds. They sing their hearts out and entertain everyone around them with their color and their music. Research, detail, and academics are more difficult for them. Finding flowing style is important, moving slowly enough with their writing to complete their thoughts and ideas.

4. *Whales and Dolphins:* These are brilliant, quiet explorers of the unconscious and psychological world. Whale and dolphin people often write science fiction or deep psychological or emotional explorations into unknown worlds, worlds that are hidden from normal view and are difficult to describe. Oftentimes they swim together for fun and to share. These writers can become too obscure. They need to discern what they're really trying to accomplish and then stick to it. They can migrate all over the map searching out new feeding grounds and swimming away too soon from their original ideas.

Do you have a sense of your inner nature as a creative person? Meditate on your creative self. How is it different from your everyday self? Spend some time looking at these categories and meditating with them. How does each category move within you? How do you express yourself and your experience of life? Your writing power animal chooses you, has chosen you long since and that is why you learn the way you do, why you move through life the way you do. Do you stalk ideas, circling them, watching them? Do you ruminate on them? Do you flit from one to the other, testing its essence, and then fly away? Do you swim deep, probing the psyche as it explores unknown worlds? Allow your writing power animal to come forward, invite it into your conscious life. A whole new world awaits you.

Some people might ask why a power animal is important as an elemental force in communication. I didn't really understand this either until I met Agnes Whistling Elk and Ruby Plenty Chiefs. Now I know that your power animal is symbolic of your original nature, so knowing your power animal is a way of knowing yourself in a very intimate and profound way.

In our society today, we live very far away from the experience of our original nature. Our conditioning transforms our lives in ways that are not congruent with the life our original nature intended for us. Discovering your power animal is a journey that leads you back home to your true self. Most of us grow up and become the person our parents wanted us to be, or we take on a persona that society dictates. Sadly, very few of us live authentic lives within the circle of power that is our true nature.

How can our communications in life be real and true if we are living from a counterfeit self, a self devised by the designs of others? Finding our power animal accesses our true nature, which is often hidden or covered up by the roles we play to please others. I teach the journey of the power animal because I know that to truly express yourself with honesty and integrity, from the voice of your spirit, you must know your original nature.

When your power animal comes to you, you will understand something very key about your own nature that perhaps you never saw. The language of each animal is unique, and it is vital to know if you are predatory by nature or if you are a grazer. People with predatory power animals like a wolf or a puma have a tendency to communicate very directly, sometimes pinning others with their eyes and their emphatic statements. A grazer, like a deer or an elk, is much subtler in communicating and will often speak softly and tentatively.

It is useful to know the power animals of others while communicating. Knowing your own power animal will help you learn how to discern the energies of the animal powers that animate another person's being. If you study the way animals live and then see a particular animal energy in another person, you will learn how to approach that person. If the person is predatory, you will know that you can speak openly and directly, whereas with someone who is a grazer you may need to take a softer, less perceptually threatening approach.

Always remember that no animal is more powerful than another, for each is a reflection of the Great Spirit. Sensing and communing with your power animal will give you access to your essence and will awaken you to a remembrance of who you truly are.

When the spirit does not work with the hand, there is no art.

—Leonardo da Vinci

# WALKING WITH STILL FEET

The world tends to support what it understands. If you are a beginning writer, this may be an idea to honor. If somebody had said this to me in the beginning, I would have said that I cannot be anything but what I am. I cannot write anything but what is true for me. Perhaps I would still say that. On the other hand, it depends on why you are writing. This reminds me of a quote from Oscar Wilde: "When bankers get together for dinner they discuss art. When artists get together for dinner they discuss money." Are you supporting a family? Are you interested in fame? What is it that you are really doing, and why are you doing it? Why did you choose to be a writer over all other things? This is a big question that needs to be answered within you.

On this earth, as we walk daily, within our creative soul, we walk before the gods that we have worshipped within ourselves, be they great painters, musicians, writers, Jesus, Buddha, or the Great Spirit. Interestingly, when you walk at the highest levels of your consciousness, then your feet will be still. You realize that there is no need for haste. You realize that your heart is full and that all of who you are breathes with a fire of creation and creativity. As you live your life, your hands, your mind, your being are busy, constantly doing and creating for an effect, for a reason, usually for survival on one level or another. When you pass on to other worlds, you return to the central fires of creation from where you have come; your ancestors, all of the beings of light and dark, are part of you. You realize that you are the center of the universe and that things in daily life on this earth mean something quite different from what you find when you walk among the gods of spirit. The gods of spirit can be the wind or the sun on a placid pond reflecting brilliant mirrors and diamonds of light into your eyes. What I am trying to say is that the urgency that we feel in our daily lives, an urgency that is also a burden and a sense of duty and a question of what really and truly matters in your life, this urgency that we feel is something to be reckoned with. You have the creativity and the power of all of the gods burning within your own soul. Whether that is expressed now or later in your life is dependent upon what it is that you are really trying to accomplish. What is your own sense of urgency? For what do you yearn most urgently?

And I need to pause at this point, and for a moment—just to myself and maybe you to yourself—whisper the names of the people whom I love in this life and how I want to serve them. With what part of myself do I want to seduce reality and make it mine? Who deserves what, and what is it that I have not owned that I need to own as far as my real life is concerned? What have you disowned in life, and what do you yet need to own? Ours is a materialistic society. A society grows out of the language its people speak; as English speakers we tend to be materialistic and

therefore pragmatic. Someone in this society may be very poetic—
and many are—but that poetry has to be found and nurtured and
loved, often without a lot of support because the poetic flight of
fancy for any writer goes into an existence that may seem very
unfamiliar to people and may be expressed differently from the
way other poets have expressed it. Therefore, there is always the
possibility that you may be accepted or you may not.

As a writer, are you also a mystic? Are you someone trying to
teach people something, or is writing simply an expression of your
love for your craft or the emotions that you are feeling? Maybe it
is not beauty and light that urge you. Maybe you feel a great
anger, and you splash that anger in some fantastic way, in some
tangled dialogue and plot that creates mystery and excitement in
people who are unfamiliar with that kind of fusion. What I am
suggesting is not to be untrue to who you are but to understand
very, very clearly why you are writing. What are you trying to impart with your writing? Perhaps you are an extremely good jour-
nalist who can describe things perfectly. Maybe you need to look
at that and see the depths of your own spirit and where you want
to go, how deeply you want to descend that ladder. Because the
ladder that you walk up is the ladder of fire coming back to the
surface, coming back to the reality of social existence.

I would like to quote from Normandi Ellis's translation of
*Awakening Osiris, The Egyptian Book of the Dead,* from the chapter
"Thoth Speaks."

> *The ibis and the ink pot—these are blessed. For as the ibis pecks
> along the bank for a bit of food, so the scribe searches among his
> thoughts for some truth to tell. All the work is his to speak, its se-
> crets written down in his heart from the beginning of time, the god's
> words rising upward through his dark belly seeking light at the edge*

*of his throat. We are made of god stuff, the explosion of stars, particles of light, molded in the presence of gods. The gods are with us. Their secrets writ only in the scrolls of men's hearts, the law of creation, death and change inscribed in the blood and seed of man's love. In the beginning and at the end, the book is opened and we see what in life we are asked to remember.* ★

And I would like to say, also, that we see what in life we are asked to do. What is it that we are intended to accomplish? That is your task, more even than the writing at hand. Think of that, please. What are you trying to accomplish in your writing?

★Normandi Ellis, *Awakening Osiris: The Egyptian Book of the Dead* (Grand Rapids, MI: Phanes Press, 1988).

You can only be dangerous when you accept your death. Then you become dangerous in spite of anything. A dangerous woman can do anything because she will do anything. A powerful woman will do the unthinkable because the unthinkable belongs to her.

—AGNES WHISTLING ELK, FROM *MEDICINE WOMAN*

# DUENDE AND THE MAGICIAN OF WORDS

When you write, are you free of walls or do you create something to push against? Heat is necessary for transformation to occur, and heat is created by some kind of friction. You can rub sticks together to ignite a fire or express a profound moment of inspiration that makes you aware of the divine force within all that lives.

But to know the creative life force, a never-ending partner must be chosen by you who is the magician of words so that your greatness can be born. Then, suddenly, within your mind and heart, without cause or effect, movement begins and you become a shape-shifter dancing the flamenco with wild spontaneity and unpracticed skill. Then the tango steps overtake you, and out of a poised, immense shadow appears your master partner, a mysterious figure that evades your grasp and remains just out of reach upon entering the dearest part of your soul. You have chosen a form of heat, the greatest partner of all: the ever-present sense of death, which leads you into the exotic dance of life and death, to the beginning of what the Andalusian artists of the southern region of Spain call *duende*. Now your world has changed forever.

The great Andalusian poet and twentieth-century dramatist Federico García Lorca spoke passionately of the *duende* in a speech he delivered in Havana, Cuba, in the 1930s after a visit to the United States, calling it the mysterious force that everyone feels and no philosopher has ever explained, a power and not a construct, a struggle and not a concept. "The *duende* will not approach at all if he does not see the possibility of death, if he is not convinced he will circle death's house, if there is not every assurance he can rustle the branches borne aloft by us all, that neither have, nor may ever have, the power to console. With idea, with sound, or with gesture, the *Duende* chooses the brim of the well for his open struggle with the creator. Angel and Muse escape in the violin or in musical measure, but the *Duende* draws blood, and in the healing of the wound that never quite closes, all that is unprecedented and invented in a man's work has its origin."

*Duende* is the ever-present sense of death, the partner from within who is the magician of words. If you watch a great flamenco dancer, or guitarist, you experience the passion within them. That passion, I believe, comes from their core spirit, which recognizes death in each moment of life. Death becomes their ally. It sits on their left shoulder, always. When death becomes your ally, you no longer have concern about self-worth because you *are* self-worth. With death as your ally, sitting on your left shoulder, you have a key to a life without superfluous fear.

*Duende* has always been in search of me, and my life has always been about life and death. Always, death has been on my left shoulder. In the beginning I would write about my feelings of sadness about death, an animal dying, a family member or a friend passing. There has always been drama and perhaps that is why my beautiful teachers have always been dramatic in the way they have taught me and led me to a certain place of awareness.

People often ask me why, when I teach, I don't put my apprentices through the same kind of life-defying situations that my teachers put me through, for example, as Zoila did when I was writing *Jaguar Woman*. In the chapter entitled *"La Caldera,"* I wrote about the time Zoila had me walk on a narrow cliff trail in the middle of the jungle, where I could have dropped to my death into a chasm with any wrong step.

There are many situations like that in my writing. I always experienced something before I would write about it. In *"La Caldera,"* I was physically and emotionally walking through my fears. When people wonder why I don't teach in the same way, I say to them that we each need a personal cache with a new fragrance, a different texture and force. It is my experience that just as every person is an individual, so too each individual has different needs, whether they be in the process of writing or in the process of spiritual evolvement. And if you want to truly teach someone, you must become willing to meet that person where he or she is and speak to the light that shines within that individual. We say that experience is the best teacher, and yet so many people say to me that they would have fallen to their deaths in *"La Caldera,"* or they would have turned around and gone back. Would you really push someone off the top of the ski slope if you knew that person didn't know how to stand on skis or use the poles to maneuver around obstacles on the slope? Not everybody has the same sense of death as I do. And if I tried to foist my awareness on them and insist that they learn only from my perspective, what kind of teacher would I be?

What inspires you? When I ask ten people, "What inspires you?" I get ten very different answers. Inspiration can come from ideas or it can come from nature, from animals, love, Central Park in New York City, from so many different things. But when I speak of writing, I must speak of *duende* because there is never a moment in my life in which there isn't a deep welling up of emotion that has been developed over a lifetime of being conscious of the fleeting moments that I embrace with this life. I could be having lunch with someone today and it may be the last time I see her, even though she is only twenty years old.

I am desperate to reach that place where my art, my craft, lives inside me. A community like Santa Fe, New Mexico, has always seemed to be the kind of place that would stimulate me, taking me back to the beginning where all roads lead. There are so many memories of my life in Santa Fe. I want to traverse those roads again in some way that is meaningful. Yet an emotional diary is not what I am interested in creating. What I am interested in is the source, the fire and what creates the fire (even though I seem to wander behind fire trucks that create water-laden fire areas now without flames, places that have been torched, lives that have been torched—wayfarers who are wandering through unforested, burned-out hillsides!). The presence of humanity helps in some ways because there is movement, action, energy moved around into dark corners where the lights have ceased shining for centuries. As Goethe said when he lay dying, "More light."

Do you feel *duende*? If you do, how do you express it in your writing? What words do you create for yourself? How does your writing portray what is precious to you? What is your gold?

I want to find and return to the source of what drives us and what that drive looks like, not the shovels and picks but the gold that still has to be discovered and dug out of the ground. Sometimes defining what that gold is, what is precious, is one of the hardest things about the search, the journey, the quest, the digging.

We make such a drama out of life. For some reason, the human being has to develop an extraordinary ego just to exist. But in fact life is simply life, and life is sacred.

—Agnes Whistling Elk, from *Shakkai, Woman of the Sacred Garden*

# "I BELIEVE BECAUSE
# IT IS ABSURD"

I believe because it is absurd." These words were written by a Christian priest named Tertullian in the second or third century A.D. They make a beautiful statement because we can become serious writers, we can become perhaps deeply religious, or we can become fanatically political, obsessed with self and very grandiose. Beliefs are a fence around our consciousness; we cannot go further than our belief structure. So perhaps it is more helpful to be aware of the divine balances and imbalances in life.

Find your humor in the absurdity of the human condition and the repetition of diabolical history. Instead of dwelling on the serious, dwell on the authentic and the unimitated in your life. The light in your soul is shining like no other, but there is a key: you have to trust yourself. Can you relax for just a moment and think back to the last time you were upset and see the other side of your frustration? No? Then try again. In fact, write a few paragraphs about your deep intensity of self. Don't you see how your ego takes hold of your conscious mind when you feel most unsure and insecure? When it comes to your ego, what does it look like? How does it feel about your writing? Do you trust yourself?

Visualize your ego as an animal or as a character in your life. Let it take on personality. Now have a conversation with it and discuss the absurdity and the seriousness of your life. Describe your ego self as the animal that you visualize. This is not the same as your writing power animal, which is symbolic of your inner nature. This is your ego animal; it represents your ego, which is often vastly different from your inner core! Remember that this dialogue is intimately about you and not about life in general. The practice of visualization connects you profoundly into your imagination.

The search for self as a writer is one of the most powerful endeavors that you face as a writer. That is why it is important to become less thought-reactive and focus more on rebirthing yourself into a brighter world of expression and thinking as you write. This occurs as you grow through your writing. When you write, you create mirrors that reflect your fears, your flaws, your strengths and talents, or the absence of what you thought you were. Through these mirrors, resistance is created and your learning begins. It's not about perfection. There is no perfection anywhere; that's a part of our belief structure that is indeed absurd. Life is a wonder and is absurd because it exists without explanation. Perfection requires explanation, does it not? Living life is about honoring your vulnerabilities. Whether you know it or not, you are entering a new world through your flaws as well as your talents, and this new world exists in a more vibrant state of mind. In creating a written page of words, which are actually symbols that mean many unexplainable things, a truth is coming to you and to those who read your words. The synchronicities begin to happen without your noticing. You will experience that you are *not* lost and that your eternal dialogue with whatever is divine to you continues no matter what.

What are your strengths? What are your frailties? What are your best and worst mirrors, those reflections of you that you find everywhere? Write them down and become intimately familiar with them, because they are the seeds for your best writing. If you were a symbol, what would it be?

What makes me read the contours of a form, the graceful or the gnarled tangle of a tree branch, as if it were my own soul blowing gently in the wind? I walk into the rise of a mountain as if traversing its height, lifting my thoughts to the sky, wanting to enter the sanctuary of light that is created there by the clouds. Do I want to leave myself entirely, gathering myself into the worship of thunder and the gods of illumination? My breakthrough will come one day in my complete detachment from the notion of perfection. The process of living absorbs my life.

Living as a writer can be exquisitely painful, chaotic, and joyous, as you already know. I see this earth walk as a learning process, a schoolhouse for discovering awareness. Do we as humans learn much without massive pain? Of course this remains debatable, but be honest with yourself. With the glow of your interior flame, does not your greatest challenge begin? Goethe's *Italian Journey* states so well—"for we sense the frightful conditions under which only the true naturals can realize the ultimate possibility of achievement." And you are a true natural.

As I wrote in my book *Medicine Woman,* when I asked my teacher Agnes, "Why me?" She answered with no hesitation, "We are all chosen, but so few have the courage to follow the call to greatness, to enlightenment, to power."

Sometimes we think we know who we are. And yet we always have a funny feeling that maybe we're not complete, that maybe there is something we're missing. Actually, what happens is that after you have been writing and working, you come to a place where you hit a bump in the road. There's a space, there's a pause, when suddenly you feel you can't go forward. You've gone through all that you know and suddenly you're empty.

What I think happens with all of us who write is that writing is a process of discovery. It is a journey into the world of who we are, the essence of who we are, and it takes that essence to finish a work of art. So when you hit this place, if you do (and you may not, because you may have always been coming from a place of who you truly are in your writing), let me explain what happens to you. When you hit this low valley and nothing is coming, you simply don't know. You don't know if you need to start a new book or if you need to keep pushing through the walls around you and the current work. When that happens to you, take a look at what you're really doing and say to yourself, "Perhaps who I really am is finally catching up to who I thought I was, and who I thought I was is finally giving space to what the truth of my character and my integrity really is so that it can express itself through this world and become known."

At that point there is a moment when you shape-shift from the writer you thought you were to the writer you *really* are, and what a magnificent moment that is. When you shape-shift into a place of higher degree—no matter what it is that you are doing (it could be what you thought your state of health was in the world and now you discover what is your real state of health)—you are at a crossroads. And these crossroads are places of power, places of superiority within your own higher self, places of creativity. You are able to realize that when you choose what is true (whatever

that is in your life and, in particular, in your writing), all of a sudden something awesome begins to happen and your writing takes
on a new shape and a new form because you begin to realize on
the deepest level of your being that you are, in fact, a thought
form who is constructed out of your very own process of thinking: what you think, you are becoming. When you think you can
do it, you can win. You will win.

Do a short exercise with yourself, if you will. When or if you
reach this plateau where suddenly nothing is coming in your writing, sit with yourself and ask yourself who is writing, and write
about that for just a little bit. Take a look at it. Meditate on it. One
of the things to do at this point is to give yourself some time. Often
when we're starting a book, we work nonstop; we empty the clay
pot of our talent and learning and wisdom. We empty it completely.

There is a process that I call gathering, and gathering is that
time when you allow yourself to research, to have silence, to be
in a place of introspection, of enjoyment, to reflect on just the
harmony of yourself. I would suggest that you start filling your
clay pot of a soul with some reading, some physical exercise,
some silence, so that you can revisit your creativity from a different perspective. You need to nourish yourself, nourish your creative process by reading, by picking out those books which
change you, poetry perhaps, aspects of philosophy, nature, some
form of beauty, music, time alone, time for yourself. And suddenly you look at that clay pot, and it is filled again with creativity and energy. You see that you've replenished yourself, your
core. Then you can begin the process of emptying once again
into your work, into your writing. You have allowed yourself the
time for nourishment.

I have seen so many writers who, once they get started on a
project, can't relax and simply allow their bodies to tell them that

it is time to take it easy for a few days. It's time to replenish, to allow yourself to rest and enjoy yourself for a short time, no work, no deadlines, maybe no phone calls. Just be with yourself. Enjoy yourself and allow yourself to find the next progression, the next direction for what you are doing. What pieces of art changed you? Now is the time to immerse yourself in them, and leave your writing alone for a little while.

Your work is to discover your work and then with all your heart to give yourself to it.  — BUDDHA

# DIVINING THE HIDDEN:
# A NOTE ABOUT SHAMANISM

Shamanism in the twenty-first century is to me a way of understanding and developing one's spiritual enlightenment. When you think that a society grows out of the language that it speaks, and you look at the English-speaking world, which is so often a pragmatic and generally materialistic society, you realize that the practice of any religious or sacred art is a difficult task.

We have very few words in our language to describe evolution into spiritual consciousness and realization. When we use a term like *shamanism,* in a sense it means something different to everyone reading it. As defined in Merriam-Webster's dictionary, the word *shaman* comes from the Tungusic language of Siberia, and is used to describe "a priest or priestess who uses magic for the purpose of curing the sick, divining the hidden, and controlling events." It has been adopted into the English language to describe a native healer who is usually born into a long line of medicine men or women and/or who is taught the healing arts from birth.

There are also other kinds of shaman healers. One is a person who is simply born with a mark, whatever that mark may be in the native tradition that the person is born to. Another is one who is born into a life situation where she nearly loses her life in some life-defying situation. This person lives through the experience and comes out on the other side with very special abilities. She is a shaman who heals differently and may not be part of a medicine tradition in any given tribe. These latter shamans are wounded healers. They are extraordinary men and women who have developed the art of Seeing; they can choreograph the energies of the universe in a way that brings healing and light into people's lives.

Every shaman is different. Every nation of Native people is different. Their guardians, their ruling icons, are vastly diversified, but the source of power is always the same. There is always the firstness of woman, the understanding that power comes from Mother Earth and Father Sky; there are always the elementals, the directions, and the unseen mysteries and powers of the other dimensions of reality.

We all as human beings are looking for the meaning of life. We all experience disease, not only of the physical body but also of the spirit. Shamans help you to balance the physical state with the spiritual, the known with the unknown. I think it is very important in this time of stress, this time of environmental disillusionment, that we understand as a people that no one owns the truth and that each and every one of us, no matter who we are, is an expression of life that is a part of the Great Spirit that animates us. This is a time that we need to reach across racial, societal, and religious barriers and join hands with our sisters and brothers to heal this planet and to heal ourselves.

Shamanism is about the end of duality. It is about oneness with all of the energies that surround you. If you do not understand the oneness of energy, you do not understand the laws of power. The first lesson of power is that we are all alone. And then there is a giant abyss between this statement and the last lesson of power, which is that we are all one. The last lesson of power is the oneness of us all, the respect and the honor given to different ideologies and thought, not war between those ideologies but honor.

People around this earth are looking desperately for the reason for life, the understanding of God in our lives. When someone is trying to find the meaning of life through the practice of ancient ritual, perhaps using drums and sage, is that person not doing what ancient peoples wanted from the beginning? The ancient peoples wanted everyone who discovered them to understand their way of life. People who are hungering to go back to the earth, to understand the shamanic harmonies of life, the magic of life, the understanding that there are physical and spiritual dimensions that can be united in a life of wholeness, are also trying to heal the earth through the process of healing themselves.

To be a shaman is very different from being interested in shamanism. A shaman has a true gift and has been touched by spirit. That person is "one-who-knows-how" in the words of my teachers. She knows how to understand the universe, how to travel in the dimensions of reality and power that most people have neither the desire nor the focus to travel. She is neither more nor less important than those who have no desire to follow this path. She simply is what she is.

The process of shamanism is a process of growth and effort and focus that brings people into balance with the world around them. It is a process of love. I am often stunned when I work with people who have become identified with the technique of their job. Our world, our society, seems to reward those who become centered on the idea of more and bigger and more powerful at all costs. Lost in that rush of effort is the artifice, the enjoyment of the process. Lost in that rush is the love for what you do. Shamanism as I have experienced it is the love of life, the profound love for healing and harmony and balance between the physical world and the world of profound joyous spirit. There is no way to explain the face of Great Spirit once you have experienced that face. You can describe how you feel when you see the face; you can describe the stillness at the center of the storm, the flowing bliss that courses through your veins. But you cannot describe the beauty that is expressed except by the love of process and the grace that comes from that.

When you think of doing your heart's desire, when you think about manifesting intent into the world, to me that is like Zen painting. If I look at a Zen painting, I feel a kind of joy. I feel uplifted. I feel my energy rise. I don't know how anyone could feel otherwise. Zen painting makes you want to play music or sing or tell everybody about what you are manifesting.

The work of a painter like Picasso is very different. His work is linear, very strong, more scientific. Modern painting is sometimes called Western painting because of the influence of technology. In a very simplistic, generalized way, the work of Picasso, Dali, Magritte seems to come more from the side of science than from the mystic soul. It is more technologically oriented, surreal in a sense, which I love because it is within the surreality that the truth of a painting lies, not in the hard, technologically correct line.

To me, however, there is no similarity between a Picasso painting and a painting by a Zen master or a shaman master. They are like two totally different worlds because they come from two totally different parts of a person. That, of course, is the reason that all artists are different, and *vive la différence!* To me, when you approach art from technology, you lose a lot of the beauty, even in the beautiful painting of a Campbell Soup can, and it's no longer helpful in bringing you, the viewer, to the place of the divine presence inside of you. Instead, it simply reflects the rather insane mind of man, which sometimes makes me feel dizzy, nauseated, and even ill.

When I approach writing, I approach it from the stance of the Zen masters. If you study a Zen painting closely, there are a few things which may be very surprising. The first thing you notice is that human figures are usually very small, and if you don't look very, very carefully, you will oftentimes miss the people that may be in the painting. The trees are big; the mountains, the landscape is huge; the sky is giant . . . and oftentimes the canvas will be empty. In Western painting, the human being is very big and covers the whole canvas. We make the person huge, and nature, the sky, very small if it is in the painting at all. It's not proportionate, and therefore it is often not a true statement. When the human being covers the whole canvas, it is very egotistical, perhaps as a reflection of the painter.

I follow the path of the Zen master who is a shaman. In the Zen master's world, as in the shaman's world, man is only a tiny part of the great universe. The mountains, the waterfalls, the sun, stars, and moon, are giant, whereas man is a tiny little piece way down in the corner, perhaps crossing a bridge. There are no Western painters who come immediately to mind whose paintings—the vision of the painter—have been surrounded by emptiness, where the earth is huge and humanity is small. It always seems to be the other way around.

When I was in Australia during the writing of *Crystal Woman,* I worked for days and days making an incredible sandpainting. And one day, Ruby Plenty Chiefs came into my *wurley* and walked right through the middle of my sandpainting. She just splashed all my sands to the four winds. I was so furious and so hurt, and I couldn't understand it, so I yelled at her. And she said, "Where is the unknown? You have no place for the unknown."

The Zen master's canvas is empty because of the immensity of the universe and also because of the immensity of possibility. Look at your writing project as an empty canvas, an empty space of possibility. When you define ahead of time exactly what it is that you want and what it is going to say, what you're going to write, then the possibilities for it to become different or expanded are lost. It would be wonderful if you could do a painting of your own life right now and what your plan for it is. What would your painting look like? How would manifestation look? How do you observe the emptiness in your life? What would you surround that emptiness with? Would you leave it open? Would it be completely without definition at all? As you approach your writing project, how does your movement into the world look? What do you need to let go of in the world in order to manifest your writing? What no longer serves you as a writer? If you have a sense of the emptiness and the hugeness of the universe of possibility in terms of what you are trying to manifest, all things become possible. You don't rule out anything because it is all bigger than you and it's already set in motion. What is the unknown aspect in your writing?

You have to set your intent, and then you have to let it happen. You can't hold on to an idea. You let the idea fly into the universe of possibility. You send it out to carry the message of your intent to the Great Spirit, and then like a carrier pigeon it returns home for more food, for the next idea. What does your painting look like now that the first message has come home? What does the space look like? What is the emptiness? What is the possibility? The possibility is the entire universe, of course, but if you're doing the painting of your writing life, you leave space not only on the painting but also within your own soul and your own mind for all possibility. Anything can happen. Whatever happens is the teaching from the Great Spirit. The Great Spirit may look at what you're trying to manifest and have a different idea altogether. You don't know, but be open to that possibility. Otherwise you miss the teaching, you miss the probability and the possibility, and all is lost.

Make a painting now, not a Zen painting but a shamanic painting of you in the world today considering the manifestation of your writing life. Paint what that is like. Bring in from the universe things that relate to that manifestation, like birds, like the messenger smoke, all the things of nature, all the beauty of nature, and how you stand in that nature. What does the unknown look like now? How do you define it? Or do you define it? What colors do you use and what do they mean to you? Bring this out of your soul, out of your heart, and out of your spirit—not out of your mind.

A shaman is usually someone who has been gifted with spirit, with the knowledge of spirit, the knowing of mystery. And you can witness in that person the years and years of study, of practice, of work to learn and hone these gifts into a laser beam of effective light that can be directed at any given disease to reconstitute a reflection of perfect light and health. A shaman has mastered his technique. A shaman has understood intimately the tools of her trade. But a shaman is not identified with those tools or with the technique because a true shaman has a perfect balance between technique and the love of the process and the art of what he or she is accomplishing to promote harmony and balance among all living things.

What does your journey as a writer look like?

Dreams are like clouds. Sometimes with power we create a great wind and clouds bump into each other. At that moment of collision something new becomes possible. You can change the agreements that you have with your reality. You can change reality.

—RUBY PLENTY CHIEFS, FROM *WINDHORSE WOMAN*

# WRITER AS MAGICIAN

There are three "attentions" of which my teachers have often spoken, three different perceptions of reality. These attentions are "first" attention, "second" attention, and "third" attention. First attention is an understanding of the physical world, an ordering of the physical world. Second attention is being able to move into an awareness and understanding of the unknown. And third attention is, quite literally, being able to organize both the world of the physical and the world of the unknown at the same time—the parallel reality that goes along with the physical reality—without losing your ability to stay grounded in one or the other.★

In writing, I see this as a very great issue because you are working in the physical world, you are writing in first attention, and

---

★Some of you may remember that Carlos Castaneda also spoke of these attentions, although from a somewhat different perspective. His books were among the first books to bring these shamanic ideas and language into the everyday world (in English).

yet you are perceiving with your intuition or your inspiration, which comes from second attention. For the writer, second attention works automatically with first attention, and it is being able to weave these two worlds together with words that gives you an understanding of third attention, a product of inspiration or intuition that is rooted in the physical world. As writer, you also understand the spaces between the words. You understand the underlying truth and the magnificence of inspiration and perhaps even other realities. You may not call it other realities; you may simply call it imagination or creativity. But you've moved between the worlds to bring back a wonderful piece of writing. You have moved into the world of power.

Try a brief experiment. Write a short paragraph from first attention, from the physical world. And then with your second attention, intuit the words or thoughts that exist *between* the words you have written. Write these words and thoughts out, perhaps as an entirely new paragraph, and then write your paragraph again. What is the feeling or intent *between* your written words?

What hooks your creativity and your imagination into the world of power, a world that is deeper and more full of interest and mystery than the ordinary world, is the ability to shift what shamans call your assemblage point. The assemblage point is a place of knowing within your body that perceives the shift between the physical world and the world that is unexplainable. For instance, life force is unexplainable. We know that a person is alive (first attention), but we don't know why. So we talk about many things that describe being alive: we talk about love, we talk about hate; we talk about murder; about enlightenment; we talk about using our ability to visualize, to image other aspects of consciousness. What do you think this is? If you truly understand these other aspects of consciousness, then you truly understand second attention. And third attention is your ability to write it all into a readable story, a readable context where people can either learn from it or be entertained in a way that is deep and powerful.

I think "writer as shaman" is an interesting statement because I think it is very real. Why? Because, as a writer, you are able to learn about, to facilitate and express, different levels of perception in a way that is understandable to other people. For your writing to be understandable to others, it has to be understandable to you. And therein lies the key. It's *your* perception of power, your perception of what is real and special to others. Writing is about *your* ability to elevate into the higher states of consciousness and understand that the creative process is an extraordinary gift. You are drinking from an exquisite fountain that is magical and filled with light, that has the prospect of giving you renewed life and renewed vitality. Write about something that changed your life. Write about something that is out of the ordinary, something unusual, something personal. Make it intimate. People learn more from being entertained than from scientific detail. Humor is more memorable than a scientist giving his theory on relativity. When you see the humor of your life, you can make fun of yourself and you can expose your flaws, and that is what makes your work entertaining and intimate on that deeper level. It is the ability to express a theory of relativity on that deeper level that carries the theory out into the world in a way that can change lives.

I've been absolutely terrified every moment of my life and I've never let it keep me from doing a single thing I wanted to do.

— GEORGIA O'KEEFFE

*11*

## POET AS MYSTIC

I believe that there are two kinds of people who create, the mystic and the poet or writer. The poet, the writer, creates in a world that is tangible, the "real world," the world that we see every day. You can read a poem, a book, a song, something that a poet creates. The mystics, however, create on the inner planes. They create in the inner world. So often you don't see what a mystic creates. You don't see paintings, for instance, by Jesus or Buddha. You read words that were written about them. You see a grace or an essence of how they express themselves. I am interested in bringing you to a place of mysticism, a place of silence within yourself where you can access the purest, highest, most elevated form of expression that exists within you. Therein lies the journey of discovery, of placing mirrors within yourself that reflect the existence around you.

We are often lost in the shadowy reflections of our social structure and our conditioning, which are so often borrowed knowledge.

It is knowledge that doesn't have the kind of brilliance and shine and insight that we are looking for. Don't you want to go somewhere in your writing where perhaps other people don't go? Don't you want to be able to take your readers to a place they may not be able to find by themselves? Perhaps, as a writer, you can change people, change meaning, give them a new perspective, and move them into a place within themselves that perhaps they couldn't find otherwise, so that they then can find the mystery, that inexplicable aspect that propels you into the depths of your creativity. I say depths instead of height because I think that it is a place that you go into deep within yourself.

*We came to a small cave and sat down. I was out of breath and dripping with perspiration. I was still miffed at Zoila and didn't say anything. She looked calm, perhaps a little bored. Sitting there, I realized how stiff I was and how many aches and pains I had. I gazed at the fantastic view across the canyon. The sky was golden. I could see the narrow path spiral upward, and I was amazed that I had managed it. Nearby, a glint of sunlight caught my eye. I stood up, and there on a ledge was a gold Mayan mask inlaid with turquoise, emerald, and jade. The stones were carved in exquisite snake and jaguar designs.*

*"Zoila, look at these gems and this mask. It's surely solid gold. Do you know why it's here?"*

*Zoila's voice had a matter-of-fact quality. "It is a beautiful trinket. You take it. It is a gift from the spirits of* la caldera.*"*

*I climbed up the almost perpendicular ledge and ran my hands over the gleaming surface of the mask, brushing away the dust.*

*"It's worth a fortune."*

*"Take it."*

*"But I can't just take it, Zoila; maybe it's here for a reason."*

*"Of course you can. You found it."*

*"But I simply can't. I don't know why, but I can't."*

*I took a final look at the gorgeous mask shimmering in the sun. The bright stones glimmered alluringly. I turned away and crawled down from the ledge. The discovery had somehow made me melancholy.*

*"Zoila, you take it. I just can't."*

*"Never," Zoila said. "Treasures belong to the one who first sees them."*★

As I said in my book *Jaguar Woman,* I could not take the beautiful jeweled mask that had been left for me. It had been left for me so that I could experience taking a most extraordinary treasure that I had discovered. And I couldn't take it. When I told Zoila to take it, she answered that treasure belongs to the one who finds it.

I have worked with Zoila's statement for years since that experience. Besides everything else that happened in *La Caldera,* I realized that I couldn't take my power. I also couldn't take an accolade or a treasure, something that was given to me because of what I had accomplished. One of the most difficult things for me was being recognized as a good writer, as someone who could tell a story, to say nothing of the fact that I was frightened to be center stage, frightened to accept a mystic quality within myself that helped me grow into being a teacher. At first it was terrifying to me, partly because I was an abused child and my instinct was to remain hidden. If I presented myself to the world, to my father, I would get hit. In a sense, I created that in my life simply because

---

★Lynn Andrews, *Jaguar Woman and the Wisdom of the Butterfly Tree* (New York: Harper & Row, 1985).

of the fear of it. That is an extraordinarily difficult thing for writers to accept. Deep inside there may be that feeling of not being worthy of recognition, not being worthy enough to write, let alone to have an extraordinary experience. If you share what is within you, you could perhaps enlighten people to their own mystery.

All of this was part of why I could not take that mask. It did not belong to me, not the physical mask itself but the jewel, the treasure that it was. I could not accept that kind of gift as an explanation to myself through the mystery, that I was beautiful and worthy of such a thing. I have deeply experienced that no matter what our belief structures, our society, our race, even our religion, we all want the same things. We want to belong. We want to be loved. We want to feel worthy. We want to have successful lives. We want our children to be happy. We want to be in touch with the divine, whatever that is to us.

I chose to take the experience of *La Caldera* and write about it but purposely leave it mysterious to the reader so that you could test yourself, test your own allies within you. Do you have the intent and the strength to take the jeweled mask? This mask represented beauty and perfection and other aspects that I couldn't deal with either. I would have felt very uncomfortable putting that mask over my very simple, plain face.

In shamanism you become a hunter first. You learn how to hunt. You learn how to hunt for knowledge and the ability to see the truth. You educate yourself about your prey, your prey being what you need to write, what you need for poetry, what you need to make yourself strong with a voice that is all your own. That takes research not only into the subject about which you are writing but into your own psyche, the mystery of your being. When you have become a true hunter, and you search and stalk and dance with energies, then you become a warrior or a warrioress. You become the shaman. You become the writer, and the writer is the one who speaks with the muses. That is the old way of the Greek world, of speaking with the muses and understanding where your voice comes from. Is it from your anger or from your love? Is it from fear, the great enemy of the warrior? What aspect of yourself is writing? Ask yourself that. Meditate on who is writing.

When you figure out who is writing, where do you feel it in your body? That is where you will find your ally or your muse. An ally in shamanism is that part of yourself that is your higher being, that part of yourself that does not feel, does not judge, but simply helps you to manifest. The muses, however, become a bridge between the divine, the mystery, and your mental capacity.

I don't know what your destiny will be, but one thing I know: The only ones among you who will be truly happy are those who have sought and found how to serve. —ALBERT SCHWEITZER

# HONORING THE MUSES

In the process of service, light comes to you. The muses gather around you; they look over your shoulder and protect you. These muses wish you to tell a story, maybe one that has never been told before. When I write a book, I have an altar, not a religious altar but an altar to the spirit of writing because the spirit of writing, the spirit of a story has stalked me for a long time and I want to honor that stalking spirit. So I light candles, and I try to understand which muses have approached.

According to Greek mythology, the Muses were nine sister goddesses born to Zeus and Mnemosyne at the foot of Mount Olympus (before his marriage to Hera), who presided over song, poetry and inspiration, and the arts and sciences. They are

Calliope, the Beautiful Voice, the fair-voiced muse, the muse of heroic and epic poetry. Her symbol: The writing tablet, and sometimes the stylus.

*Clio, the Proclaimer,* muse of history and heroic poetry. Her symbol: The parchment scroll.

*Erato, the Lovely Muse,* muse of love poems. Her symbol: the lyre.

*Euterpe, the Delight or Giver of Pleasure,* muse of lyric poetry and music. Her symbol: the flute.

*Melpomene, the Songstress of Tragedy.* Her symbol: the tragic mask.

*Polyhymnia, She of Many Hymns,* muse of sacred poetry and hymn. Her symbol: the pensive or meditative look.

*Terpsichore, the Whirler,* muse of dancing and dramatic chorus. She is often shown seated or dancing with the lyre.

*Thalia, the Flourishing Muse,* is the muse of comedy, who wears the comic mask.

*Urania, the Heavenly Muse,* muse of astronomy and sometimes astrology as symbolized by the celestial globe.

Worship of the Muses evolved from the idea that they governed song, poetry, and inspiration. They gained in popularity during the Renaissance, with references to them appearing in plays, sonnets, and paintings. Libations of milk, honey, and water were poured out when honoring them. When a Greek was about to work on any kind of creative endeavor, the Muses were always called in and a ceremony was done. You can do this, too. Find your muse and simply light a candle for her. You can rename the muses if you like, and light a different colored candle for each. And then light a candle for the story on which you are working. Light a candle for your story and honor it, just as you honor the muses. Place blessings on your altar if you have one, prayer sticks for what you are accomplishing and for the great gift of creativity that has found you. Perhaps take a ritual bath and meditate. Petition the muses, for you are now in service to them, sometimes to one, sometimes to many. They are wonderful to work with.

Our muses are a little different in our modern world. They come from the female, I believe, because this is a female planet, Mother Earth. The strength of expression comes through your ally, through the male, Father Sun. But Mother Earth is the one who brings us into true relationship with the God-self, who births the muses out of our ability to use memory, to forget things that get in our way.

I talk a lot about God-self, the divine, becoming a warrior. Writing is a journey. You can look at writing in many ways. You can look at it from the technical perspective—grammar, syntax, plot, characters, and so forth. You can also look at what you are writing as a story line that perhaps has been stalking you for a long time, maybe your whole life. You have a sense that there is an energy circling you, and it comes up again and again.

In the beginning, I wanted to write something that would educate, that would do away with ignorance and lift people out of a place of paralysis, out of mentation and the rational body. I wanted to move readers out of that place and into something more speculative, into a mystery of swirling light within which they would find their own synchronicity and ability to pick out what is valuable. When I met Agnes Whistling Elk and Ruby Plenty Chiefs, I realized that I had to write about my experiences. I wrote *Medicine Woman* not thinking, really, about publishing it. I wrote it for the women and their sacred dream. I wrote it in honor of who they were and my experiences with them. I felt that it was an honor to present them with a manuscript that they had asked me to write.

I went to stay with Agnes for a couple of years because she had asked me to come. I arrived in Canada with no money, my house rented out. Arriving in the middle of the night I ran to her cabin. But Agnes was doing a very strange thing. She was sitting out by a little fire. She looked up at me with very cold eyes and said, "What are you doing here? You're not Indian."

I was instantly crushed.

I said, "But you invited me to stay."

"Oh, no," she said, "you don't belong here. Go."

"Go?"

"Yes, go and write the first of many manuscripts about our work and life together." She was very pompous. Then she stood up and lifted her fingers to the sky, which was full of dark shadows and lightning. "Lift your spirit, little one, and take what you have learned about the ancient and sacred ways of woman to your people. Share it. Tell them."

"How am I supposed to do that, Agnes," I said, tears rolling down my face. "You told me that this was secret, that I wasn't supposed to tell anyone about you. Now I'm supposed to go home and stand on a soapbox?" I was so angry and felt so manipulated.

"You go and you write about our work and our dreaming together. Do not return until it is finished. We will not see you or dream you until you are done." She turned her back on me, not even allowing me to spend the night.

She did an interesting thing here, something that for many years I hadn't really understood. She was making me furious so that I had the strength, the anger to actually accomplish the task. I had been a dilettante, one of those people who couldn't really complete a work from beginning to middle to end. I would start something and then go on to the next thing before the first thing was finished. That was a serious flaw that I had never seen in myself. I felt that I had done my homework. I had studied many different things in my life, but the one basic thing that I really needed to deal with, I hadn't. That was the fact that I couldn't finish what I had started.

So I left Canada and went home. But I didn't have all my crutches, those things that I depended on, like my telephone and my friends. I had to move away to a little cabin I finally found, and began to write. I went through my shaman death, which means that I lost a sense of my ego. That threw me into terrifying fields of energy that I didn't understand. But I went through it. I had a very strong will, a great curiosity, and I wanted to learn. I was also innocent, which Agnes said is the reason I made it through at all. She said that it was because of my innocence that I was actually able to complete the manuscript. It took me a long time to write *Medicine Woman*. In the writing of it, I created a mirror so that I could see myself thoroughly, deeply, and fully.

Writing is a mirror. Remember that. Oftentimes, you don't want to look in the mirror because the mirror seems distorted. You can't believe that what you see reflected is actually your true self. You think you look much better than what is reflected back. But it is in the flaws that beauty is often found. I have spoken about Ginevee, the Aboriginal woman in Australia who taught me so much. One day she held up a crystal to the sun and the light reflected through the crystal, creating prisms of rainbow light that flashed across the ground. She said, "There, crystals are like humans. It is the flaw within that crystal that is creating the rainbow beauty that you see all over the ground. It is within our flaws that our beauty comes. Honor your flaws. Celebrate them. They mark your path on this earthwalk. These flaws of yours create the beauty that you are trying to find. You know it's there. Understand your flaws. Look at them. Go into the center of them. With your writing, you will come up against every flaw that you have. See them as markers along the trail. They mark the crossroads through which discernment, sacred will, and intent will be found and exercised."

*Marriage is in many ways a simplification of life, and it naturally combines the strengths and wills of two young people so that, together, they seem to reach farther into the future than they did before. Above all, marriage is a new task and a new seriousness—a new demand on the strength and generosity of each partner, and a great new danger for both.*

*The point of marriage is not to create a quick commonality by tearing down all boundaries; on the contrary, a good marriage is one in which each partner appoints the other to be the guardian of their solitude, and thus they show each other the greatest possible trust. A merging of two people is an impossibility, and where it seems to exist, it is a hemming-in, a mutual consent that robs one party or both parties of their fullest freedom and development. But once the realization is accepted that even between the closest people infinite distances exist, a marvelous living side by side can grow up for them, if they succeed in loving the expanse between them, which gives them the possibility of always seeing each other as a whole and before an immense sky.*

*That is why this too must be the criterion for rejection or choice: whether you are willing to stand guard over someone else's solitude, and whether you are able to set this same person at the gate of your own depths, which he learns of only through what steps forth, in holiday clothing, out of the great darkness.*

*Life is self-transformation, and human relationships, which are an extract of life, are the most changeable of all, they rise and fall from minute to minute, and lovers are those for whom no moment is like any other. People between whom nothing habitual ever takes place, nothing that has already existed, but just what is new, unexpected, unprecedented. There are such connections, which must be a very great, an almost unbearable happiness, but they can occur only between very rich beings, between those who have become, each for his own sake, rich, calm, and concentrated; only if two worlds are wide and deep and individual can they be combined. . . . For the more we are, the richer everything we experience is. And those who want to have a deep love in their lives must collect and save for it, and gather honey.*

*Within this sacred circle of your spiritual family and friends the two of you have chosen to stand together, to bring together your spirit shields to fly in harmony throughout this lifetime. So it is with your blessing and with our love that we welcome you to our circle now as husband and wife.* ★

Writer and muse—one with the blessing of the universe. Form a marriage with your muse. Become the guardian of each other's solitude so that you can grow side by side and allow your story to be birthed from this bond. Celebrate this marriage just as you would celebrate a marriage in the flesh, for from it will come all the grace and magnificence that you have ever dreamed your writing could be. You are the mystic. You are the poet. You are the warrior, the hunter. You are a writer in service to the written word.

---

★Rainer Maria Rilke, *Letters to a Young Poet,* translated and with a foreword by Stephen Mitchell (New York: Vintage Books, 1984).

We were all born wild like a mountain lion, and to live in civilization
we become sheep at a very young age. We become tame. But we are
not house pets. We are fierce and wild by nature.

—TWIN DREAMERS, FROM *STAR WOMAN*

## KNOW YOUR ALLY

It is often said by my teachers and by other shamans whom I
have met in the world that you are only as powerful as your ally.
Your ally is a magnificent inspiration that comes through your
passion and other aspects of your emotional body. Your ally
comes when you begin to work. It looks over your shoulder and
is curious, wanting to see what you are doing. Then it begins to
flutter its wings. It begins to ignite your fire from within. This is
a wonderful experience.

There is energy that resides inside you that can teach you glo-
rious things about truth and power, about the grandeur of exquisite descriptions, of fragrances, sounds, vistas, and other symbols in
the realm of the senses that belong to you in the depths of your
soul. By finding these hidden energies and exploring their forms,
you become acquainted with your creative ally.

There is another way to acquaint yourself with your ally. If you
have a pain in your knee, for example, I have found that often there

is an ally present within you that wants to be heard. Oftentimes it can create pain in your body to attract your attention. I teach many methods for working with energy forms, or allies. One very effective way is to quiet yourself and your mind and breathe deeply. Close your eyes, focus your consciousness in your knee area, and move inside your pain. Most likely the pain will start to move around, like mercury under your finger. Keep following it. You will see a form taking shape. Concentrate and see the form your ally is taking. The pain is formed because your ally needs your awareness. So listen and discover what it has to tell you about yourself and your quality of writing. What have you been avoiding? Why can't you move forward?

It is the same way with your writing. You have inspiration that comes to you from the ethers, and the ally makes a way for the unknown to become known. But if you don't begin writing, the inspiration will leave you. An ally, however, is always somewhere near you. It wants to be recognized. Allies are energy forms that assist you and help you to open gateways that can transform your writing. They help you find the seeds from which your creativity was meant to sprout.

Your ally is with you no matter what you are doing. Your ally has no wisdom. It has no knowledge. But it does have the ability to give you strength and help empower you toward whatever it is you wish to do. An ally is a bridge between the unconscious and the conscious worlds. Now you can understand why people say that a shaman is only as powerful as his ally. That applies to writing as well. A writer is only as powerful as his or her ally. This means that you need spiritual endurance as well as physical endurance to be able to complete a task.

What do I mean by spiritual endurance? Spiritual endurance means that you have the strength, the commitment, the will to explore creative realms. It is oftentimes like a divine will to do your homework. You do your research. You make a foundation for yourself as a writer. You go to the university of the spirit, so to speak, and find out who you are and who is writing. You take time to meditate on that. Who *is* it that is writing? Who *is* it that is expressing herself or needs to express herself within your writing? Who *is* it, indeed, who is searching the universe for that beam of light, that opening of a fantastic vision or gateway within which you begin to travel and wander as if you have opened your eyes for the very first time?

You find your ally by moving into your "bush soul," your writer's spirit. In my book *Crystal Woman,* I wrote about Ginevee, a beautiful Aboriginal woman of Australia. In her everyday activities, Ginevee was always involved in some aspect of the sacred, whether she was dreaming in the sacred dreamtime and doing ceremony or making a fire and preparing a meal. She was always in communication with the mystery, with the life force that we can't explain but know is there. We know we are alive, but what makes us alive is part of the mystery. The knowing is what Aboriginal shamans call the "bush soul." I want to help you find your "bush soul," your soul as a writer. When you find your soul as a writer, you find your voice. It is hard to find a voice when you have laryngitis and you can't speak. It is hard to fly if you have already clipped your wings before you have begun. It is hard to find your creativity without an experience of your innermost secrets.

Writing is much more than sitting down with pen and paper. It is the process of psychology related to the spirit. It is almost a process of "not-doing," so that your creative soul can become active. The ancient Chinese explained beautifully how a conscious thought unites with the unconscious to become an act of doing *without our preconception* of the doing. You consider making a work of art. If you are a painter, you consider the painting. You consider the paintbrush and the paint. As a writer, you consider your book or your story. But at this point your masterpiece isn't ready to become a finished object. You work with yourself and your materials, until one moment you pick up the brush and place it in the paint. Then the canvas becomes immaterial to the brush and paint. Suddenly, something comes through you and the act becomes reality and you create something. That something becomes a painting or a body of writing. You realize on a final stroke or sentence that you have been in the "zone," or what I would see as a mystical connection from the unconscious to the conscious, from the ethers of the sacred dream, of the "bush soul," into your artistry. An idea, a color, an act, a physical body is transformed into something more than you ever dreamed of.

The ally is an important part of this process. The ally gives you an unconscious direction and strength, which sometimes you follow and sometimes you misread. The communication between you and your ally is essential, however, for this whole act to occur.

How do you communicate with something you cannot see? Ginevee worked so deeply with me in the dreamtime to help me understand this process. She would come to me with an idea. She wouldn't say the idea, but I would feel it from her. I would see it in her eyes, and she would ask me for one word. I would say something like "light" or "movement." Then the two of us would set out across the outback, covered with grease and ashes from the fire and red ochre, each of us carrying a dilly bag. It may have been storming or very cold or very, very hot. Ginevee would stop occasionally and ask me for another word, always turning me inside to my spirit. Then she would find some colored earth and place it on my face or somewhere on my body in streaks and colors and textures. She would ask me to put the same colors on her, sometimes around her eyes or around her mouth. We were alone in a great wilderness with no one to disturb us. We had no television, no telephone, and no belongings. Yet we felt as if the universe belonged to us, that we were in communication with the greatest of beings, unseen yet hiding behind spinifex grass or the boulders and peeking out to smile or sing to us.

After hours of silence, sometimes I would say to her that I had lost my song. I would be deeply depressed because I was struggling so hard to understand this unknown world of mystery that was being wrapped around me like a sacred blanket. I could not see it. But I could not disrobe myself from it. Sometimes it would hem me in too closely, as if my arms were being held down and I was becoming so heavy that I could barely walk.

"You can never lose your song," Ginevee would say to me. This was the dreamtime knocking at my invisible door, trying to get me to wake up, trying to get me to let go of delusions that no longer healed me or served me. Then I finally experienced the power of a word. In the beginning was the word. Of course, I thought perhaps words and language came from nature as a way of communing with the higher soul and the primal source of power.

For me, finding the ally became a process of letting go of everything I knew. To require you to do that sitting at your desk somewhere in the world is a lot to ask. But I am asking you to do that in order to be a great writer, to find the essence of the words that you are writing and the knowing that words are symbols. Language is a very fine and beautiful way to communicate. When you truly communicate through language, you must find the juice between the words, and then you drink of that juice. When you drink of that juice, you begin to fly and move the most important aspects of your creative work.

I think you have a responsibility not only to yourself but also to your expression, to the words that you use and how you find them. An ally can help you with that. It's like sweeping up your conceptual floor. It's gathering all of your research into a sacred bundle and wearing it around your neck with words streaming out as you catch them and look at them like forms. Like beautiful crystals, you gather them and put them in your sacred medicine bundle of literacy. The bundle grows, becoming bigger, and you write. The allies give you the strength to do that. What a magical process! What a magical bridge you become between the physical world and the world of inspiration.

Ruby Plenty Chiefs, one of my great mentors, would often say to me, "Blah, blah, blah, blah, blah." She would say with a wry laugh, "Why do you talk so much and say so little?" Hemingway had a wonderful way of describing events and people. He would very carefully paint out all the words in his work that were not effective, that were not needed.

That is what the allies do. They help you to hone what you are doing in a very special way so that you do not waste your energy. But first you have to find and get to know your ally. The ally has actually been with you all of your life, perhaps through an object that you held as a child, a toy or a teddy bear, or from something special to you, like an old leather binding on a book of Dante that you would run your fingers over and feel the drama and the words lifting up from the worn pages inside. For me, it was sitting up in the apple tree and writing. Writing became a great ally as I began my life as a shaman, much the same as my other ally, the wolf, curled up at my feet like my dog. I would sense this wolf's voracious hunger to learn and to teach and to give over that teaching to others.

Find out where your ally lives in your body. It may be somewhere that you are unaware of, maybe in your heart or in your feet. Maybe that is why you need to walk to think. Find where your ally lives. Your ally wants to speak to you, wants to give to you, but you have to give your ally an opening. When I was walking in the outback of Australia with Ginevee, she would ask me to open to anything new. As an example, we were three days away from camp and walking through a beautiful, desolate area of red earth. There was no water in the creeks. The trees were gnarled, old and gray. We were walking and walking and walking.

Finally, she sat down and said, "Here. We will stay here. It is good."

I said, "I must have water." We weren't carrying canteens. We were using an old primitive way of carrying water called a *coolamon*, dug out of a tree root and balanced on top of our heads. Mine was a beautiful piece of hollowed-out wood that I had painted with swirling designs and edged with the sap from spinifex grass to create something that I could carry water in. It was Ginevee's idea. Ginevee wanted us to do this, to be in the old way. She carried a large *coolamon* on her head. It was much harder for me to balance my smaller one on my head without spilling. With her as a wonderful guide, I was trying very intently to understand how to survive in the outback, although she really didn't give me a lot of direction. She let me fail and heal and fail and heal.

Finally I stumbled over a dead fall of branches, dumped my water, sat down on the red sand, and started to cry. I thought, "I can't go any farther." I had no water and hadn't eaten in days. Ginevee indicated that we were going to dig for *witchiti* grubs. Then she rolled away a rock and there, like magic, was a watering hole called a billabong. We gathered water from that hidden spring. I hoped that it was healthy water, and it was. I was so obsessed with survival that I forgot that Ginevee had something to teach me. I thought that she had forgotten my spirit.

As we prepared camp, we built a fire and a small *wurley,* a half-round basketlike structure out of spinifex grass and twigs to shelter us from the cold wind that would come up in the late afternoon. After digging for grubs and roasting them over the fire on a stick, like chitlins, I learned that if I'm hungry enough, I will eat anything! After eating, I really wasn't thinking about spiritual teachings. I wasn't thinking of anything except staying warm. We went to sleep that night lying back to back, waking up every half hour to move wood into the fire. Sometime near dawn, I felt the ground shake and I awoke startled and frightened, as people in a war zone must be frightened when bombs suddenly drop. There was an incredible sound and shaking of the earth's surface. I leaped up, as did Ginevee. She pulled me behind an outcropping of rocks as a herd of wild camels tromped through the camp at a gallop. I was in awe of these beings, the light of the moon shimmering on their coats and in their wild eyes. They made strange noises. The ground continued to shake, and Ginevee whispered in my ear, "See, it's a quickening. Ha. A quickening."

The camels were suddenly gone from sight. I looked after them in the silence, my body shaking.

"A quickening. When a woman of power comes to you like ghost camels wild in the night, you must quicken to keep up with her."

A woman of power to me is like writing—finding the allies, feeling your muses, and you quicken to your inspiration. You become more. You stretch and you agonize and try to distract yourself. But there is no real distraction from your destiny because your story has stalked you for a long time and finally it's getting tired of waiting. It's quickening you to catch up with it: Come on! Find the facility, the ability to write what you need! That is when you seek out your ally. As you find it, you begin to see that your ally is indeed peeking over your shoulder. You may think you are alone writing in a café in Paris, but now there is a crowd around you. There are muses and your ally, and the dreamtime of your imagination, sacred and golden.

That night with Ginevee, we moved into the dreamtime, or a deeply altered state of consciousness. She took my hand and we lifted our spirits off the ground as if we were on a magic blanket, a sacred *ronga* that holds the sacred designs of the people. We floated up above the outback and into the universe around Australia, where we met both exquisite and fearsome beings of the parallel reality called the dreamtime. Many were reflections of my own fears and trepidation, many held the wonderment that makes me real and makes this world a place that has meaning. The meaning was taught to me and I wrote about it in *Crystal Woman*.

As a writer, I began to look at my words as floating out of the mouths of gods and warriors like myself, like you, you who have the courage to come up against yourself, to see yourself in the mirror. At first you may see yourself as unworthy, and then as a warrior so worthy that you take your power and run with it. You run to the edges of the horizons in the universe. You might say, "I just want to write a book about flowers or cooking." Even in writing about the simplest acts and things, build your foundation, learn your craft. And then you have a magical moment in your life, an epiphany. You may touch thousands of people with your version of that epiphany. Take a look at *Zen and the Art of Motorcycle Maintenance* by Robert Pirsig or *Golf in the Kingdom* by Michael

Murphy, who wrote about finding spirit and truth in an athletic experience that might have seemed very ordinary and unrelated to the process of creative activity.

I came to Ginevee with extraordinary curiosity and the will to learn. Perhaps the key was innocence and respect. Ginevee, a small dark-skinned woman of high degree, was as foreign to me as buffalo in a rain forest. When I arrived in her village, the people took everything from me that represented my world—my suit-cases, my clothes, everything disappeared but my tennis shoes be-cause my feet were tender and uncalloused. All that I knew of my world was discarded. I was a surreal being in her existence and therefore a great source of humor for her, and for me as well! I never doubted. I never judged. I was open and pure to her per-ception, to what she wanted to teach me and gift me with.

In a sense, your story, your act of creation is an unknown world, just as an Aboriginal woman in the outback of Australia was un-known to me. You must follow and trust and push beyond your terrors. The billabong, the life-sustaining water in the middle of a barren desert, suddenly appears to you and you roll away the rock that has hidden it from your view. Your writing spirit is like that water, a life-sustaining aquifer deep beneath the earth, hidden in your creative soul until you find it.

Ginevee knew the trail. I trusted and followed her without ques-tion, wearing ashes and grease and colors from the earth. In a sense, you wear the colors of your native creation. You wander through the mysteries of the outback with your Ginevee and your creative will. Never doubt this, or you will surely perish. Your ally walks with you. If you listen, if you feel, if you encour-age yourself, your ally honors you and will help you find your way through the most forbidden terrain.

The etymological root of the word desire is *desirer,* which means holding your star or following your star. When you are rooted in your desire, a desire that is available only to you, when you have accepted who you truly are, then you are following your star. You are following that magnificent, shining, radiant star that is always leading you toward your destiny.

"I wish I knew the beauty of leaves falling. To whom are we beautiful as we go?" Holding up images of conflicting opposites that are held together through the imagination is one way of seeing what the ally does for you. It allows you to have the strength to compare, define, and war with conflicting aspects of yourself.

And yet, as Carlos Castaneda wrote in *Don Juan,* when you find your ally, you have to test that ally. You as a writer have to test your ally or conflicting aspects within yourself. There are a lot of influences floating around in the universe and you want to be sure this really is your ally living in your body or in the energy field around you, in your emotions, in your dream body, or in your lucid night dreaming. Somewhere your ally is very close to you, and you'll be aware of its presence. You cannot avoid the ally.

Finally, as Don Juan taught Carlos, you have to take hold of your ally and hold it symbolically by the neck, hold it down so that it finally and at last gives you its power. Maybe it doesn't want to give you its power. Then you will have to take power, which is a statement I made in *Medicine Woman,* which some people have misunderstood. They thought that what I meant was that you have to steal power from someone else.

Red Dog the sorcerer, about whom I wrote so extensively in *Medicine Woman,* was for me a teacher—a very, very difficult teacher. But he was never my ally. One way to consider the *teachers* in our lives is to see what defines that teacher. If darkness defines the light and your teacher is made of light, then there is also a predominant darkness that walks behind that teacher. That darkness can be a great teacher as well, so long as you don't look at it too long. If you look at darkness for too long, the darkness will begin to take you. Red Dog was a great teacher for me in that way. I had to learn about him. I tracked him. I observed his habits, hidden in the shadows watching him so that I could then steal back what had been stolen from us, the Marriage Basket. In order to do that, I had to feel what obsessed him, what interested him. I had to know even what he ate and when he slept. I took a very close look, and I was almost seduced by his power. I had to dip my toe deep into the pond to learn not to fall, and then I had to regain my balance before I drowned. There is a dark side to writing as well. When Truman Capote dug into the murder in his book *In Cold Blood*, surely he was horrified at the darkness but fascinated as well. We are always fascinated by the dark mysteries we do not understand. We often weave stories around them hoping to escape with our creative lives. As in the power of initiation, writing about the dark side teaches you and awakens you and makes you very aware of your need for respect of that which does not kill you.

Remember that your ally is a magnificent inspiration that comes through your passion; it is an energy form that walks within you and will help you find your way. It is the ally that can lead you out of the terrain of darkness if you have followed darkness too far. What I meant in *Medicine Woman* when I said you have to take your power is that you have to face, confront, witness your ally, and then you take the *ally*'s power because that is the relationship that is intended. The ally is asking you to prove yourself. The ally needs to know that you know how to fight and are powerful enough to understand that process.

Become conscious of the ally, feel its energy in your body, see your ally and work with its power to make it your ally in your writing.

To compose you need enlightenment. But this comes only from hard work; there's no way to stumble upon it.

—Wei Qingzhi, Poets' Jade Splinters, translated by
Tony Barnstone and Chon Ping

# 14

# POSSESSION

Do you feel possessed by your writing? Oftentimes, I feel possessed by what I call my song, the song of the story or the story itself. But oftentimes the ally tries to possess me. We need a lot of help when we are writing. We separate from people so that we have time for solitude, to create.

It is a different flow for writers who also have to make a living in the world. They have only certain days, certain times, when they can write. If that is so for you, then there are days when you go on with your regular life and days when you do your writing.

When you do your writing, do you feel obsessed with the characters, with the story line? Remember that once a story is begun, it must always be resolved. That applies to the story line of your life as well. What is the story line of your life? Write it, and then ask yourself how it feels to you. The Aborigines call this a song line or song. Once a story line is begun, a resolution must follow. You cannot very successfully begin story after story. You need to write a beginning, middle, and end, because a story, like you, is alive. This is where the aspect of testing your ally comes in. If you feel that you need to free yourself from a feeling of obsession, it could be the ally obsessing you. Maybe you don't want to be obsessed—you just want to have a pleasant experience. Similarly, the mind is a great tool, but it does not possess you; you possess the mind. An ally belongs to you and exists because of you.

An ally will test you to see what you are made of, as will a teacher, as will power. I often say in my work with people, when they have some difficulty, "That's power testing you." For instance, a woman I have recently worked with would become ill whenever she was beginning a new project. Of course, the illness takes her power away from what she is doing and distracts her completely, and she never finishes. In learning about the fact that she is made of energy and has an ally and power, two great sources of energy that are with her and help animate her creativity, she began to resolve her fear and her illness disappeared.

Most often there is a reason for us moving into the frailties of who we are, usually to distract ourselves and to sabotage the very thing that we are trying to accomplish. In the mix of all of this is the ally. Power is also in there. You are asking for power when you become the creator, because there is a side of creation that is very destructive. You transform a thought or a material into something new. You change lead into gold. It's an alchemy. When you get into the world of writing and life becomes magic and you tug on your own bootstraps to survive and express yourself as no one ever has, you are testing power. Power then tests you back. That test is a competition of wits that you are going to win, because if you don't win, then you are a loser. So you have to win, because that's why you were born.

Someone may ask you the difference between power and an ally. Power is a primal force that can work through the ally. I have seen an ally make a person very possessed with his own self-importance. For instance, someone gets extraordinary inspiration, becomes well known for it, and then becomes obsessed with his own power. What that kind of obsession really comes from is his own weakness or lack of self-esteem.

You may think that you own the words that you scribe. But to acquire them you must hear them, read them out loud, even perform them. When you know the consequences of their sound and rhythm, then they become yours. From the experiences of your life come gestation periods when you wander the earth gathering fruits, and you begin to live in a place within yourself that I call the sacred witness. You simply observe and perfect the art of seeing beyond your normal capabilities. You become fluid, you feel the bright earth living within your stimulated senses, and you begin to dream in ways you never thought possible. That is how you find and kindle your imagination and begin to truly write.

Possession is an odd term, an interesting term. In a spiritual sense, it is very negative in its context and can create great harm to someone. And yet we talk about being possessed by our writing or by a story. In a sense, that is true. I think that when a story has stalked me in the past, I shape-shift into another person for the telling of the story. And that doesn't change, really, until the story is finished. At the point that our story is finished I think we tend to find that we don't want to end the book because we have enjoyed being possessed.

For want of a better term, perhaps we could use the words "excitement," or "fascination," or "spontaneity," something that conveys the feeling of great highs and great lows, of feeling ecstasy and then the depths of depression. Yet it is also fun, it is an opening to a new experience. It is certainly not boring. Writers by nature do not want to be bored. There is nothing worse. Boredom, of course, comes from being bound up within your self. We always think it's because there are no interesting people around, or because the world has gone crazy and we can't relate to anybody anymore, or because we have lost interest in the hypnosis in which the world seems to be lost.

What a magnificent gift it is to be a writer because in being a writer you can be a step back or a step forward, away from the chaos of our cities, our belief structures, our politics. You can choose when to write. What a beautiful life if you can look at your writing life like that—the gift that it is, the extraordinary ability that it takes, and the lifestyle that it provides.

There is no question that the complexity of our life is a cause for great sleep, where we simply tune out, zone out to the real questions of survival in a state of higher consciousness, which all of us really want to do at times. But how could anyone look at life and not want to become better at it? Ask yourself, how many things have you accomplished, perhaps survived, in your life? Think of your childhood. In my childhood, for instance, I survived an incredibly difficult, challenging existence, in particular with my father, who went into levels of manic depression and rage. I was usually the brunt of his rage because I was an only child. I was very lonely. My mother, as brilliant and magnificent as she was, was very reserved with me. She loved me, she made me feel loved, she certainly cared for me, but she didn't know how to communicate with that side of me that was depressed because of my father's relationship with me. This is not an uncommon story, yet it had great impact upon me as a writer.

Look at what you have lived through and how wonderful it is

that you can look back at it now and hopefully see that everything that has occurred has been a challenge, a great challenge to your life, and you have overcome it in some way. You can write about it in your characters. I think life as a writer is innocence, as I've said now many times. It's also life as a mystic, as a shaman, as a person of high degree. A person of high degree is a description, really, of an Aboriginal warrior shaman who has special abilities to move into the dreamtime, to gather knowledge, and then give away everything and become a wise one. In a way, I see writing from that vantage point. We become a person of high degree because of our discipline. I hesitate to use the word *discipline* because it sounds like exercising at a gym—not that that's bad, because I do that all the time. But I think when looking at your life as a writer, it is a joyous celebration of your talent and of the bliss with which you become very intimately acquainted. A person of high degree in Australia is of that kind of timber.

I remember when I was finishing *Crystal Woman* in Australia and I wanted to give the camp, the village, a wonderful gift, and I didn't quite know what would be appropriate because they had all the medicine things that they needed and everything else that they needed. Even though they had so little, they didn't want more. I spoke to Ginevee, who has been such a significant teacher to me, and finally after much discussion I went and took out a radio that I had, and I gave it to them. We were all sitting in a circle. These people, you've got to understand, had never been touched by the West. They knew almost nothing of our lives. They saw it in the dreamtime, but they never really understood the chaos and the role of media in our lives. And so I gave them the radio and thought, "They're going to have fun with this." I turned the radio on, and Beethoven's Fifth flooded the *wurley* with music, and they were fascinated. They kept testing the airwaves, looking at this radio and holding it, and looking underneath it and in back of it, as you would expect someone to do who has never heard a radio, wondering where this magnificent sound was coming from. And finally, after several hours of my explanation, they gave it back to me. They didn't want it. Ginevee and one of the elders of the village said to me that they didn't want the distraction of it, that it would take them away from their more sacred life, even though it was wonderful and they appreciated it very much. They were very intent on not hurting my feelings.

I thought then and I think even more strongly now that writing, the arts of any kind, is like that radio: we have to know which dials to turn for the music to come across the airwaves. If you don't know how to press a button, how to switch on your creative life inside you, if you don't know how to allow yourself to be open to inspiration, then it is simply not going to be there.

I think differently from Ginevee and her village. I think it's important—since we chose to be born onto this earth plane knowing that it is a schoolhouse, a place for us to learn; since we chose to born into the life of a very pragmatic, materialistic English-speaking nation (realizing that a society grows out of the language its people speak)—it's important to understand and accept where we are. We have chosen this world at this time, so let's make the best of it; let's learn everything that we can learn. It's that curiosity, I think in the end, that fills us with an innocence and a wisdom that is irreplaceable, and we have a chance in this lifetime to do that. So, turn the dials within yourself. Listen to Beethoven's Fifth. Listen to the magnificent works of art that have been produced by other people, and then move into silence and your ability to be very still. And enjoy the magnificence and the incredible journey that a writer's life provides.

Surrealism is an interesting subject for writing. Some people write science fiction; some people write in a way that supports one aspect of reality superimposed on another aspect, and the connection is very surreal and misty. A friend of mine in San Francisco was a great poet, Philip Lamantia. He wrote a wonderful phrase, "flight of the seventh moon," after which I named my second book, *Flight of the Seventh Moon*. The phrase meant one thing in the context of my writing and another in the context of his writing, but it is a very surreal connection.

Lamantia spoke with me about the seven moons of the Pleiades, or the Seven Sisters. We were strolling along a quay in New Orleans at night. We were there for the American Booksellers Association convention. Allen Ginsberg and many poets and writers from around the world were there. Warner Books was giving a gathering for me, honoring our new contract at that time. Lamantia always approached life from an oblique stance that startled and inspired me. He watched the moon reflecting on the water on that humid, sultry night and saw goddesses floating from the stars, and he felt a longing to escape from himself, about which Juan Ramón Jiménez, "the martyr of beauty," also wrote in *Lorca and Jiménez, Selected Poems:* "Through work we define ourselves, and upon our work we leave our image. It is part of who we are and who we shall become."

I saw the spinning shields from the Pleiades reflecting their light and wisdom in the form of watery abstract designs. We both saw seven images in a surreal way that defined our conversation together and yet stood in juxtaposition to the reality that clamored around us soaked in wet heat and weighted air. He saw a flight in the seven moons that led us to a whole new conversation about black holes and narcissism. I saw the flight of the seven moons as shields of knowledge, flying to us from the Sisterhood of the Shields. "We are nothing but wanderers in orbit. We can never reach an end, never reach ourselves unless the end is, simply, to run after ourselves."★

Surrealism is a very efficient way of bringing the mystery that exists between the lines of your writing into a place where you can see even more, on a physical level, on an imaginative level, what it is that you are trying to give to your readers. Surrealism is certainly a translation of reality, and everybody has a different translation for whatever reality it is that we perceive. Surrealism gives us a bridge into the mystery, into the color and texture and fabric of an idea, into its fragrance, in a way that perhaps nothing else can. So take a look at the surreal qualities of someone like Philip Lamantia or Juan Ramón Jiménez, "my only two weapons, time and silence." Take a look at the surrealism of Dali or René Magritte in their painting. Look at how, in studying a Dali painting, you can ask yourself, "Is it romantic? Baroque? Stylistic? Science fiction?" Or would you describe it as it relates to your life as a whole, maybe to your life as a child, maybe to your life, for instance, as a writer?

---

★*Lorca and Jiménez, Selected Poems*, Robert Bly, ed. (Boston: Beacon Press, 1997).

I publish a piece in order to kill it, so that I won't have to fool around with it any longer.  —WILLIAM GASS

# BEGINNINGS AND ENDINGS

Many writers talk about how to begin a work. They have writer's block. They can't get going.

I would like to talk about how to end a book, which is equally important. Years ago I would place all the chapters I had written on a clothesline, and I would see that under the different headings I had put out as a working outline there were certain areas that were skimpy. Always, now, I work on the Sacred Wheel.

*The Sacred Wheel is a paradigm for the process of mind, and it is especially helpful when working with abstract concepts [such as conceptualizing a book from beginning to end!]. If we take a simple wheel and divide it like a compass into four directions, we have physicality and manifestation in the South, transformation and emotions in the West, spirit in the North, and mind in the East. When we use the paradigm of the Wheel, we learn to look at life from a circular perspective to see the wholeness in life."★*

---

★Lynn Andrews, *Love and Power Journal* (Carlsbad, CA: Hay House, 1999).

I use the Wheel to see the wholeness in my writing. There are other teachings of the Sacred Wheel, which you will discover in the chapter "Wheel of the Writer's Spirit." But this is the essence of movement around the Wheel, that each direction provides you with mirrors that give a particular reflection of your writing because of what that direction relates to. Our task as writers is to find balance and wholeness in our writing, and the Writer's Wheel is the way that I do that.

Before I consider a piece of writing finished, I look at how I have filled out the South, the physical aspect of preparing the homework for my book, how that has progressed and if it is now complete.

Then I look to the West at the emotions, the dream, and how to choose my story line. I see if I have followed it all the way through to a conclusion that makes sense and has meaning, that has suspense and is fulfilling to the subject. Did you properly describe the dream in your book? When I say "the dream," I mean the dream that you have of how this book should feel and look, what it is that you want to say. Have you done that?

Then I go to the North and look at my book spiritually. Perhaps you are not a spiritual person, but most likely as a writer you have a deep sense of nature or beauty or excitement and enthusiasm and inspiration. How has that played out in your work? Has it been dispersed throughout? Have you been able to bring a balance between the South, the physical aspect of actually writing of your book, and the North, spiritual aspects that you want to explain? See if there is balance between the physical and the spiritual.

Now move to the East on the Wheel and ask yourself if the meaning is there. Is it rationally understandable? For me, this is a big aspect because I do a lot of writing in the North and the West. I look across the Wheel to the West, to the dream of my book, the emotions that are portrayed, and I must make sure that

# The Writer's Wheel

**North**
Home of Spirit
Wisdom
Strength and courage
Inspiration

**West**
Home of woman,
the female
Great Dreaming Bear,
the Sacred Dream
Emotions
Death, rebirth, and
transformation

**Center**
Self

**East**
Place of illumination
Home of man, the male
Humor
Mind
Testing to see what is real

**South**
Home of the child
Physical manifestation
Trust and innocence

the East—the wisdom of my book or my characters—is concrete, strong, and fulfilled, as well. There should be a very rational bottom line that pulls through all the characters, like a stream glowing in the sunlight, pulling the characters and the story in an understandable level all through my book to the very end.

The end comes when you have completed the South, West, North, and East on the Wheel. Then you go to the Center, to you the writer. You look at the life flow, this stream that has pulled through the book. Does it accurately represent the life flow that you feel all the way through? Remember that any story once begun must be resolved. In the writing of your story, you need to find the outcome. It is the treasure within your work. Have you found that treasure and have you imparted that to the reader? Have you brought it home to your readers to share with them in a very accurate, beautiful way? That is when the glow of your particular abilities shows the most clearly. That's when you end your book.

After I have finished a book by going through the spell check and looking at the way the words lie on the pages, I realize with some regret that I am finished. That is when I know that the book is ended. When you have finished a book, it is like a friend's leaving town and you don't know if he is ever going to return. It is hard to let go of that friend; it is hard to let go of your book. Many writers hang on to the work, thinking they need to rewrite it when it does not need to be rewritten. When it gets to a publisher, there will be many changes and shifting of sentences, anyway. When I finish a book, I don't want to let go of it either. It is like my children, my friends, it is beautiful and sweet and has caused me a great amount of pain. Like raising a teenager, you forgive your book and love it even more.

After I had finished writing *Medicine Woman,* Agnes taught me how to "give away" a book. I remember it well, because it meant a great deal to me. It is a very important aspect of the writing. It is ceremony. We were sitting together under a tree, listening to the wind laugh and sing in the branches above. I held my book securely on my lap so that it wouldn't fly away. Before going to the tree, Agnes had me cut six-inch squares of cloth out of an old shirt. She showed me how to make the squares into small pouches and fill them with tobacco mixed with other herbs, then tie each pouch with colored ribbons representing the South, the North, the West, and the East. Then, after getting two of my feathers, we took the book and bundles out under a tree.

*As I described in* Spirit Woman,

*Agnes spread out her medicine blanket and we sat on it across from each other. She took out her pipe and prayed to the four directions, the Great Spirit, and the powers of the universe and the Grandparents, and asked them to hear me in my giveaway. I smoked the pipe. Then Agnes cut a small piece of her hair and mine and we put that in a bundle, tying it with red ribbon.*

*She laughed. "That is in case I had any hold on your book," she said. "Give me your hand." Holding it, she pierced my finger with the sharp point of her hunting knife. I winced.*

*"Now smudge the front and back cover of your book with blood. Pray to release her from you and to let her grow now and find her own way. She is now separate from you. It is good." I laid the book back down and Agnes sang in Cree. Emotion welled up in me and I began to cry. I realized that I had felt something like a mother with her child. Agnes had me tie all the bundles to the feathers. After we had said our final words and rolled up the blanket, she told me to go up on the road to the crossroads and to tie the entire bundle to the branch of a tree where I would be sure someone would find and take it. It did not matter who took it, or if the spirit of the tree took it.*

*Soon it was done.*★

---

★Lynn Andrews, *Flight of the Seventh Moon* (San Francisco: Harper & Row, 1984).

Dreams pass into the reality of action. From the action stems the dream again; and this interdependence produces the highest form of living. —Anaïs Nin

# WALKABOUT

Oftentimes in writing, I find myself in a tunnel or a cave. I wander through a dark labyrinth. I try to find my gait of power, that place within myself where I can walk in the dark with my eyes wide open and see perfectly. I call this a walkabout, a rhythm, my way of moving through the darkness and the mystery of my mind and my ideas without really knowing where my next step will lead me. But I step anyway. And in that gait of power is a knowingness that has to do intimately with my belief and trust in myself and my own ability to navigate through unknown territory. It is very much like walking out into an unknown landscape, which I have done often in my life, bushwhacking my way up a mountain when there is no trail to follow or when I don't choose to follow someone else's trail. I don't stop at every sound or every strange footing that I come to; I keep on going. When bushes are in my way, I let them stroke me as I walk through them. I see the bushes as living things that are caressing my talent and my ability to endure. And when I am moving through the mysteries of my mind, I see a contradiction as another living thing that is caressing my talent and my ability to survive.

There is spiritual endurance and there is ordinary endurance. Ordinary endurance is your physical acumen, getting yourself physically strong. In my spiritual work, I have always placed a great deal of emphasis on being physically fit, on living in harmony with my body as well as with my environment. That is an important part of our work as writers, as well. Most writers sit and talk and type or write; many don't do a lot of physical activity. I do a great deal of walking in the physical world, especially when an idea is stalking me. I call on my muses during the process of walking, for in walking comes movement, particularly the movement of ideas. I am not talking about power walking. I am talking about a walkabout, moving slowly down a trail whether with my physical body or in my mind, so that my whole body becomes invested in the pursuit of the unknown. In this process, the unknown becomes known because it begins to flow through me. I don't stop that flow with any kind of "trying," physically or mentally. I don't try to describe. I just allow thoughts to flow, knowing that later on I can find my way back up the trail; later on I can edit.

Allow yourself to move out into nature and see the light on the trees, hear the sounds of the birds and the wind. Wind is spirit. Which wind direction is your ally? Is it the west wind or the north wind, the south wind or the east? They all mean something different. What do they mean to you? The west wind and the clouds can help you in your dreaming. When you sit somewhere under a tree and watch the clouds moving slowly above you, you can imagine with the power of your mind and the power of your heart and the power of your dreaming body what it would be like to be floating on those clouds. Oftentimes, the clouds become dark underneath, gray, black, and purple with lightning and the sounds of thunder. Then a beam of light comes through those clouds and shines in your eyes. Walk up those beams of light, radiant and warm. Move up to the surface of the clouds on the other side, the side that you cannot see. The side that is invisible to you is often where dreaming begins. Begin to dance with that feeling. Live with it. Join it.

Every day look for new clouds and thunderheads in the sky. Watch as they gather and become dark and heavy and eventually rain down upon you. Watch the drops as they touch the dust of the earth, bringing back its fertility. Watch as the grass reaches up toward that life-giving rain. Perhaps that rain is coming to you from a different part of the earth. Maybe it came from South America, from China, from Europe or Africa. It may be the same water that rained on Napoleon's head when he marched into Waterloo. Dream about North America before the Europeans came here. Dream of thousands of buffalo running across the plains, rain dropping on their heads, their fur, their backs. The buffalo become joyous in the rain, loving the wind on their faces and combing through their fur, reminding them of times when they were young and being cared for by the Mother. Think of the rain that may have been with you long before, in another time when you were so happy. That time may be like it is now. Rest on the clouds and dream with them. Go where they take you. They take you to the Sky Father and then the rain drops out from beneath you and the clouds disappear as they come back to earth to be rejoined with Mother Earth.

How do I as one person move beyond the pain that I see everywhere in the world, and move into joy? How do we find the joy and the bliss of existence that the mystics in the Himalayas and in every country in the world have seen, experienced, and shared over millennia? I was so excited with the 2004 Olympics, with the beautiful organization of it, the celebration of the history of Greece with the backdrop of the ancient temples standing for the beauty of the human spirit. Every person who found his or her way to that event has worked hard for a lifetime to perfect an art. Olympic athletes become the best in their fields, and they are celebrated for it. They haven't killed anybody. They don't have one belief structure that destroys another. These Olympians are in pursuit of the excellence of their own being and their own magnificent bodies.

Isn't that a statement for us all? All nations competed at the Olympics. All nations were as proud of their losses and their commitment to excellence as they were of winning. There was camaraderie, laughter, crying, sadness, joy, everything exhibited on the playing fields. Whether on horseback or bicycle, in the boxing ring or on a playing field, each of the athletes represented a different country not out of ugliness or war power but out of effort and intent and worthiness. We give prizes in the Olympics to those who are worthy of that accolade. It was beautiful to see, beautiful young people at the very height of their efforts. Not mediocre. Not angry. Not pulling down institutions, but celebrating the wondrousness of the human being. And isn't that a wonderful thing to write about?

All of life in all its forms should be celebrated, all aspects of beauty, all aspects of pain, the downtrodden and the successful. We draw interesting lines today in a country where anything is supposed to be possible. This country was founded on possibility not being taken away from anyone, from any walk of life, from the immigrant to the established family. So what is our view now in our writing? What are we celebrating? I think this is something to ask ourselves as writers. What is the history of your family? How did you come here, out of what kind of circumstances? And how does that affect what you do? Do you bring light and beauty into the shadows of life? Because for all the light that there is, there certainly are shadows. So what do you bring to the aspect of shadow? Where does your point of view place you on the Wheel? Is your passion balanced with your mind?

Is there an aspect of you that wants to bring down the world around you because of anger? I think that's a very important thing to look at because if it is true, then are you really a politician using the pen or are you a writer wanting to influence politics? Something to look at within yourself. I think this is important because the core, the source, of who you are becomes the beacon for others. And you have a responsibility for what you do as a writer because words have extraordinary power. How many times have you read a critique in a newspaper, any newspaper, and believed it? Somebody says something horrible about some actor or actress, some writer or artist. Because it is in print, you believe it: *Hmm,* there must be something here that is true, it's in print, isn't it? It's been published. Is that what you really want? What is the spiritual thrust or intention of what you do? I think that is a good question to ask yourself. And are you accomplishing what you want to do?

Oftentimes, I look at the elements when I write a book. I think to myself, is this a book that works with the element of water? Is this a book that works with the element of earth, of air, of sky? And within this process a new perspective becomes clear to me.

If I am writing about the emotions, I oftentimes move to a place of water and I image the rain bouncing off the road in front of me, making rivulets of silver and the patina of gray on the surface of the water. I think of the ocean crashing in, ebbing and surging toward the shore, placid, great depths of the sea with a whole world of life beneath the surface. Anaïs Nin wrote a novel many years ago called *Seduction of the Minotaur*. And she told me that she used an image of the planets, the stars, the moon, and the sun in regard to relationships. She took the distance between the planets and the stars to symbolize the distance between people, between lovers when they come together, and how difficult it is to go into the force field of another being of life and become one with that being, or even to travel in the same orbit as that being.

When you think about your relationships in a story, your characters, there are so many ways to look at the separation, the conflict and then the closeness between these characters. Look symbolically at the rain coming down and pelting the ground in a hurricane, the winds twisting the trees and circling through massive weather patterns. We as human beings are not unlike that. We become caught in an electrical storm and we fall in love, not understanding oftentimes what has possessed us. When you write of this, think of lightning flashes hitting a mountaintop or a home ignited in flames, home, perhaps, being the symbol for the mind. Think of the elements, of the earth. The earth is solid and slow and deep, and it perseveres through all the storms. Maybe the water flows over its surface, moves great boulders in its path, and then sinks into the earth. The earth holds the rain to its breast deep inside, nourishes the plants and all living things. The elements also fall naturally around the sacred Wheel.

In the East, where you have fire, the fire of the mind, the fire of thought, the cauldron of transformation, look at the way we transform when we meet someone meaningful in our lives. We completely transform, sometimes never to be the same again. Fire awakens us, warms us, heats our food and warms our homes, warms our bodies. Fire can destroy us and everything that we have in a very short time. Fire is dangerous, like love, like passion. How do your characters fit into these descriptions?

If you go to the North, to the air and what comes from the sky, you find inspiration and the spirit of a relationship. Relationships inspire us, not only to our depths but to great accomplishment. The air that we breathe is Spirit. If we know how to breathe properly, we become balanced in body and spirit between the world of the physical and the world of spiritual enlightenment. Where does your relationship fit in this context? In your book, with inspiration that is perhaps drawn from the environment around your character, is your character a young Donald Trump who turns to gold everything he touches? Does he enlighten or destroy? In a sense, that character may come out of the air because in a way the character is an inspiration. Even someone twisted, like a murderer, has a reason, an inspiration deep inside that makes him feel he has to do something. He may be possessed by a feeling from the West, which is emotion, but oftentimes he is also possessed by an idea from the East, by a thought that has fallen out of the ethers and ruled his life maybe since he was a child. Maybe his childhood was very abusive and it twisted him beyond repair; maybe it was educational and supportive and he sees reality through a different lens. Maybe your character thinks she is Mary Magdalene, and to make everything right in the world she has to destroy her mother or other people who are doing things that she thinks are against her religion or the deities in which she believes. This comes from the ethers into a person's soul. It may be twisted and convoluted, but it is very real to that person even though it may be difficult to explain. This is the challenge you face as the writer. How did Truman Capote fit the bizarre and tragic puzzle of *In Cold Blood* into a coherent, gripping story?

In the North is also the one who brings prayer, who brings beautiful simple devotion, maybe to Mother Nature, maybe to a set of ideals. Look at your characters. Who is a North person, a spirit person? Who are the ones who are inspired in one direction or another to change the world around them, to bring movement into your story from an almost unexplainable force?

In the West is the element of water, along with dreams. What is the dream of your story? Agnes Whistling Elk has pointed out to me many times in our work together that we are made of 90 percent water, so our emotions are symbolized by water not only in our bodies but in the rains, the streams and the lakes, the deep quiet ponds and the ocean. We are also made of our dreams, life, death, transformation, and rebirth. Oftentimes we experience many little deaths as in the change of a relationship. The acting out of an emotion is a little death in a way that can change us forever. Big deaths, of course, truly alter our consciousness.

The ability to work with the elements, with the four directions, is so very valuable to us as writers. How does this watery emotion, this thunder, this passion, this love, this hatred, fit with your slower, quieter reflection in the pond? The earth, which is in the South, holds the memories of all those who've walked before us. In the East is the mind, rationale, fire, transformation by alchemy, the reaction of one person upon another. The air in the North moves across the great earth plains and the mountains, creating beautiful windswept landscapes that undulate throughout your book, throughout your story, throughout your poems. The essence is in the air, in the North. The quality of the movement is shown on the earth and in the waters and in the fire. Air can blow out the fire. Water puts out fire. Air can also fan the fires. The fire is created on the earth somewhere. So all of the elements fitted together create a situation, each element very different from the others, with a different quality, a different texture, a different essence, a different soul.

The soul of the earth is deep, slow, full of memories. Perhaps that is why I gain so much in my walkabouts on her. The spirit of the sea, of the waters is a splash, a drop, a flow. It reflects your face and your characters. It reflects the spirit to itself so that it begins to know of itself. Fire burns the soul and the spirit. And yet it is of the same nature as the spirit of mind, the rationale, the choreography of mental stimulation and reaction and action. You think a plot into being. You add fire to it, action, depth, horror, beauty, all of which are fueled by the fire of the mind and spirit. And air breathes life into your story. If your story cannot breathe, if there is too much clutter in your story, the air cannot flow freely from one character to another. How do they breathe, each of these characters? Imagine right now, how would they breathe? Do they breathe up in the top of their lungs, very shallow? Or do they breathe mysteriously, like the memories of the earth? Does your story breathe like a wild animal, like a cheetah running after its prey across the Kalahari of Africa?

Take a look, write it down. If you want to write it down on a Wheel, which is how I would do it, put the earth in the South of the Wheel, air in the North, water in the West across from the East, which is the mind. In all that I have been telling you, balance spirit in the North (air) with physical self in the South (earth), and balance the memories of the cells of the ancestors in the South with the inspiration of the gods and the muses in the North. There is a movement between the North and the South. If your writing is to have a truth and a clarity to it, there must be movement from North to South and back to North, from East to West and West to East. Emotions in the West and mind in the East complement each other. You can't have too much emotion without rationale or too much mind without emotion, or you and your story are in trouble.

I hope you can see how magnificent your writing can truly be with the aid of the elements and the animals and your intent and your incredible abilities to describe character in the depths of all that they are. We are all in the circle. We all live on this earth; we are all a part of this earth and the sky and the waters, the fire and the air and the stones and the mountains. As the first lesson of power says, we are all alone just as a mountain stands alone over the plains. And yet, the last lesson of power is that we are all one, that in all of these elements, all of this beingness there is a oneness and we cannot be separate. For a work of art to be whole, it has to have unity. I hope I have described that unity in a way that is unusual to you so that it can be used by you in your own way to find a deeper, more interesting source than you may have seen before in your own work.

Our universe is magnificent in its manifestations of power, but when you go to the center, when you go to the beginning of things, you move, not out into the world for your instruction, but to the interior world, the universe that lives within. It is from the essence of that universe that all life is born.

—LYNN ANDREWS, *SHAKKAI, WOMAN OF THE SACRED GARDEN*

# WHEEL OF THE WRITER'S SPIRIT

W hen I look at my own body of work, I realize that the most powerful thing I have learned in my forty years of writing is the Wheel of the Writer's Spirit. This consists of a four-directional cross like this, "+", contained within a circle, which loosely illustrates the fact that in creation there is no beginning and no end.

Just as the Sacred Wheel (discussed in chapter 15) is a paradigm for the process of mind, the Wheel of the Writer's Spirit and the directional cross within it present a paradigm for the process of the creative mind. I designed this wheel because it is an invaluable tool, giving a writer, or any creative person, a form with which to build a composition. As I am sure you have experienced, creative impulses and ideas are a cohesive force that can be manipulated like a lump of clay or carefully pulled together like pieces of a puzzle. One of the best ways to organize your writing material is around the Wheel of the Writer's Spirit.

The Writer's Wheel is also a great organizing principle for defining your relationships with your ally. In your book, talk to your ally as a creative person. Within yourself, the creative person *is* your ally. And this ally can be difficult at times; it can even create an opposing force. To get on track, you may have to wrestle with your ally to make him work for you, because he tests you from time to time. So try putting your relationship with your ally on a Writer's Wheel and see if that doesn't help you.

As a shaman healer and teacher, I work with the Sacred Wheel because I believe our natural spirit is embodied around it. There is the wheel of life, there is the medicine wheel, and there is the Sacred Wheel. I work with the Sacred Wheel, and all of my other wheels grow from it. As a writer, the ability to go to the center of the Wheel of the Writer's Spirit and examine what you say is a gift. You sit in the center of the Wheel and look to the South, the world of physical manifestation. Then you look to the West, moving clockwise or sunwise around the Wheel because that is the direction our DNA spins and this gives you strength. You look to the West, the home of dreams and emotions. Then you look to the North, to the place of spirit, wisdom, and inspiration; and finally you look to the East, home of the mind, illumination, humor, and testing all that is to find out what is true for you.

If you are first beginning any work of writing, be it a book, magazine article, screenplay, personal journal, or newspaper column—even e-mail and letters—have some fun exploring your creative landscape and the source of your writing motivation from the center of the circle. Then, approximate the four directions physically, actually, and in real time. Sit down facing South, with the North behind you.

In the South, you find earth, the world of physical manifestations. So, when you are preparing your altar and your research, asking yourself how many chapters this work will have and who your audience will be, you are preparing your ground, your earth, your way of relating the harmonies of Mother Earth to your writing. You are also manifesting your dream. What you dream in the North, you manifest in the South. The South is the physical aspect of your writing; your words are valuable, but people are not going to read them unless you get them out there.

In going South first, you are also going to your physical structure, the physicality of yourself. You ask yourself whether you have done your research. Do you have an agent? An editor? Are you working with someone? Who is your sounding board? Think about the physical things that you do and determine the strengths and the weaknesses that are there. Allies live in the Center with you. You sit in the Center of your Wheel and look at the ally from the physical aspects of the South. How does the ally physically affect you? As a writer, I hope you are in good shape. If you are not, you need to learn how your ally can assist you physically. What do you need to know to be physically comfortable? Ask your ally. How do you nurture yourself and how does your ally help? What do you want to surround yourself with in physical terms, what objects? Create, for instance, an altar, a room filled with pictures, things that encourage you and books that inspire you. Create a writer's space. That's big.

When you move to the West of the Wheel, you move from earth to water. The West represents life and death. In the West are your emotions, and what you imagine your book to be at the emotional level. Also in the West is the Great Dreaming Bear that hibernates in the winter and brings you dreams, the dream of your book. You move into emotions, into the flow of the sacred dream, death and rebirth, and transformation. The West is the sacred dream and emotion, the female side of your book. How are you going to write this book from an emotional standpoint?

Your mind lives in the East and is the editor. The West, though, seems to be the source of it all in terms of content, and it's very, very important. So, you start accessing plot, setting, characters, and their feelings about one another in the West. What do your characters look like? How do they talk? What do their voices sound like? What are their dreams and how do they differ from each other? How do they contact one another? Do they love or hate each other? Do they support one another? If you are writing about something that seems more simplistic, like a romance novel or even an e-mail, envision how you feel about yourself and how you feel about the other person, the recipient of the e-mail or the character in the novel. How does your ally, who does not judge or really feel, empower you? I don't think that anyone should ever be writing *to* readers per se. Instead, what are you magnetizing from yourself? Write down the words that the West, your overall dream, brings out in you. The West brings the emotions and the feelings that will go down in your book as words. You write from the place of the West and understand what it is in your characters. You want to look at your characters from around the entire Wheel: What do they look like? Where do they live? What do their houses look like? Who are their family, and so forth. In the West, you look at what the emotional makeup is. Is your character a murderer? Is he a lover? What are his feelings about life and death? Emotionally, look at your characters.

Then you look in the North to see what the characters are like spiritually. You go to spirit, to wisdom, to your inspiration. Spirit lives in the North. Magnification of spirit is in the North. So ask yourself, "How do I find my inspiration?" Do you do that by walking in nature, as I do? Do you do that by study? By research? Where do your characters get their inspiration? Maybe they are gamblers or mystics; they get their inspiration from poker or from God. What is the wisdom of this book? Why are you writing it in the first place, and what is your spiritual viewpoint?

After you look at the person you have created, you decide what blows her skirts up? What makes her empowered? You move to the East, to the mental aspects of your book, which balance the emotions of the West. The East is where you begin to define someone, when you try to tear your character apart. This is where the left brain comes in, the masculine, the analytical self. You may decide that your character has absolutely no substance. You look at the character himself from the East. This is the place of rationality, of the mental male, and the wise old one within you. How does your character use his mind, or is he totally lost in the West of his emotions? Is he too rational? What you are doing here is narrowing the range, because the circle implies that there are other people, other characters involved who need to balance one another in some way.

I hope you see the physical setup, the emotional and mental kickoff of this stage, and where the inspiration and spirit come from to inform you. Then, *voilà,* a finished product! To me, that is the writing process in a circular state around the Wheel.

How do you find the spirit in your writing? In the North and in the Center, you are looking at two different categories. One is what you are known for and what people expect of you, people who admire you and your efforts as well as people who have no idea who you are. There is a second group of people also involved, and this is the group to whom you are broadening. That second group asks how you put spirit into writing, whatever you imagine spirit to be. You may be writing a mystery novel or a romance or something which you feel is quite simple, and you don't really think of it as a sacred piece. But if you feel your writing must have life, then you also feel that it must have spirit. For instance, take a look at Dan Brown's book *The DaVinci Code,* which is so successful. It is a murder mystery, but it is also a journey into the mystery of spirit. That's why, in my opinion, it has become so successful. It grabs you. It has juice at many levels. It can be read as a mystery novel or it can be read at a deeper level if you wish. You can say that this book of fiction really is the truth or that it is not the truth, and you've got an argument. And that's good. That's what this is about.

Many writers suddenly realize that the soul of a piece of writing is what puts depth into it. An interesting thing for you to do is to see if the pieces of your book, your vignettes, can find a structure. If you have a circle with which to work, you know that you have a beginning, a middle, and an end. It makes for a very handy structure and it happens to work creatively. I wonder how your pieces might be if you were to label them "South," "North," "West," and "East"? These pieces that you have written in some kind of macro state, pieces of inspiration you wrote perhaps without even realizing it, fit them around the Wheel in those directions. If you wander throughout your book, revelations will just kind of present themselves. It is like wandering down a trail and all at once beauty appears. You know things will not come every day, you just find them in your writing like jewels and try to figure out if they belong to you or not. Reread your work and consider whether your whole theme has been vividly developed. Have you really seen that word or phrase or idea? Did you set it up and find it defined, or does it need more development?

## Soul of Writing Wheel

**IN SEARCH OF THE HOLY GRAIL:**
*THE DaVINCI CODE*

**North**
*Characters from the book:*
*Silas the assassin, DaVinci himself*
Spiritual reaction
Spiritual guidance
Faith murders
Spiritual hope for truth
Power of female mysticism
Inspiration and clues
Black Madonna

**West**
*Character from the book:*
*Sophie Neveu*
Dream of life, death and
transformation
The trail of Mary Magdalene
and her daughter, Sara
Emotions about church
and religions
Feelings and dreams about
another reality
Emotional reaction
(fascination with mystery)

**Center**
In search of the
Holy Grail:
*The DaVinci Code*

**East**
*Characters from the book:*
*The Church hierarchy,*
*the mercenaries, the bank,*
*Capt. Fache and the police, Teabing*
Church, science, and academia
The Bible, Nag Hamadi,
and other findings
Reasoning the credibility of the
Christ and the Holy Grail
Intellectual diversity and
questioning of truth
Mental reaction
Need to be right

**South**
*Character from the book:*
*Professor Langdon*
Physical search
Ancient dream
The Bible, Nag Hamadi, etc.
Symbolism
Secrecy and intrigue
Physical reaction (greed)

I'd like you to experiment with the wonderful, many-faceted *DaVinci Code* by Dan Brown. I put this book on my Writer's Wheel from the approach of finding the soul of that work. This is what I found. How would you change or add to this Wheel? Try finding the soul of your own work on the Wheel.

The whole concept of allies—where do you think that belongs in your book? If you were to put this on a Wheel, the ally would be in the center with you; it's part of your intent, your power. Maybe that's where your book begins, in the Center, working with the circle and looking out at the East, West, North, and South. The ally is your power to create, your work of art. As a visual device, you can start with the center, visualize that center, and cluster the vignettes or pieces of writing around the Wheel. Then keep adding to the Center, to the West, the East, the North, and the South—the five pieces of the Wheel, the five sections in your book, each with its own graphic. By the time you reach the end of the book, you will see a full circle, which is like putting the shards together. It's a vessel. By definition, the graphic becomes its own. It is as if we were sitting on a mountain that houses a monastery; you look out to the south and clouds drift over, the vignettes are like little shards that cast their own shadows in a certain way. The vignettes each have their own character and meaning, and each sheds light. You do this around the entire circle until it is complete. And then you've got it! It is right in the sense that it gives you a form with which to work.

I think what happens to so many writers is that they don't believe in themselves. The Writer's Wheel gives you something from which to work, from which to lift off, although I don't want it to become a paradigm which you feel you absolutely have to follow, something that stifles your work or your creativity. Action produces results, and the Wheel provides a way for you to take action. It gives you a way to go, a way to look at yourself, your work, your agent, publisher, and everything else. The Wheel starts with you at the center, the place of power. Inspiration oftentimes will come after you actually start writing. But first you must know how to steer your ship, find the wheel of your ship. You then become aware of the flow and the current and the tides. Are you in shallow water at a particular place in your book? This might be an interesting way to approach it. This is the wheel of life and how you find a safe harbor. That harbor is the work that actually flows properly, it is being able to cruise in a sea or a lake. As captain of this ship, you have to find a safe harbor.

Rough seas, where you think you are going to sink, are also part of the process. Shallow waters are where you become stuck, thinking you might run aground. Wind you can't control, but you can control the sails. Writer's block is akin to running abeach. Each and every vignette or piece you write can be placed on the Wheel by itself. There are emotional, physical, spiritual, and mental barriers to everything; there are various ways to go. Call upon your ally. Your ally is at the center. Your ally is the strength to get you on to the creative process. Your ally is the energy, but you are the one who steers the ship. The ally does not steer the ship.

It seems to me that if you are looking to the South at this point, to the physical, then emotionally you may be stuck. Mentally you may be telling yourself that you cannot do it; you are telling yourself scary stories so that you can't function. It is also in the South that you tell yourself you don't have enough money to be a writer or that you get too exhausted working at other jobs to do your writing. It's tied up with recognition and finances. You feel pain when you're not recognized, when you feel that no matter what you do, nobody is going to like it. I think that if you put each thing on the Wheel, you will see how each aspect, all of the energy, flows in all of the directions. And this is cool!

If you put all of the things on the Wheel, in what order do you have them? It doesn't matter. But each person rewrites the book as he reads it. You take each piece and say, "Oh gosh, what are my barriers as a writer?" You may say, "I'm an emotional mess. I am blocking myself through my emotions." Or you may find that you are so mental that you can't find any reason why anybody would read this book, so why write it? That kind of thing.

When I write a book, I approach it from a paradigm for the process of mind that is the Sacred Wheel. I don't want to write my books like anybody else. I want to take you into *my* world, the world of spirit and soul. I want to take you into that place of God-given talent, of expression and creativity. When I talk about my writing, I am really speaking of a spiritual process that brings me closer to the creative source in the universe. To me, that creative source is the Great Spirit, similar to one's God, Goddess Mother, Great Earth Mother. The creative source of the universe is the oneness within the self, where all languages are spoken and all things are written long before we are born and will continue to be so long after we pass on.

I wonder about the charisma that some actors and some writers have, a charisma that is unexplainable, that is beyond skill and beyond technical ability. It is a charisma that is oozing out of their pores like a passionate bright energy, possibly an unused clairvoyance for all creative impulses that move in ways unnamed through all living things. There are people in this world who can perceive unknown forces of energy and use them without even knowing what they do. They use these energies, perceive them, and "download" them if you will. Sometimes these people love themselves; often they are frightened because so many others are frightened by them. They see so much more reality than most. These people are often writers, poets. They are the shamans of our time, and yet so often they are troubled because they know not what to do with the specialness that they are.

That is why I use the Sacred Wheel when I approach my writing. Movement around this Wheel is about the transformation of the creative process. Where does this book come from inside me as a feeling and a thinking person? How do I put my arms around my book? What does it feel like to my senses, my eyes, my hearing, my voice, my heart, my soul? Intuitive inspiration is Spirit to me. How do I dance with Spirit in my book? How do I hear Spirit? Does Spirit even want me to write this book?

Is my book a spirit book? Or is it a material book? Is it written for my soul and the souls of others (in the North), or is it written for other reasons, say to impart important information (in the East)? Perhaps I want to instruct people and ground them in the manifestation of their intuitive world or the manifestation of money.

How wonderful it is to be asked the question, "How does a shaman write a book?" To me it comes from a magical spirit within one's deepest self. Think of all the books that are written today: Harry Potter, screenplays like *The Matrix,* and so on. There are so many writings that are talking about other aspects of higher being. What extraordinary opportunity there is today to move into a place of heightened reality and perception. When somebody comes to me to explore the possibility of publishing his or her writing, moving their writing into a place of readable and accessible power, I begin to read what they have written and I wait for the writing to change me, to move me into a place where the spirit of process begins to wake up, a place where the dream suddenly becomes accessible, where windows open and sunlight, air, and breezes blow into the darker recesses of my mind. I wait to see if a curtain lifts.

There are four directions on the Sacred Wheel: the South, the West, the North, and the East. Within each of these directions are elements or aspects of nature.

## THE WRITER'S WHEEL EXPLAINED: DIRECTIONAL CROSS OF THE WRITER'S SPIRIT

Like a mouse with its nose close to the ground, an animal symbol positioned and living in the south of the Sacred Wheel, I would like to take you around the Writer's Wheel. I would like to show you how to balance your writing and your book in a new and perhaps different way from what you had thought of before. You draw a circle for this Writer's Wheel, a wheel for yourself, something that represents the circle of life for you.

In the South of the Wheel, you nest like the mouse in a very sacred way. In the shamanic tradition, a mouse is no less powerful than a buffalo. Its powers are simply different. The mouse has its nose close to the ground. It knows the rhythms of Mother Earth as well as anyone. When you nest like the mouse, you are very careful. You nest in a way that is protected from predators. You circle around and gather things. For a writer, you are gathering information. You are gathering words. You are gathering what you need to be comfortable in your writing space. That space may be very sparse with just a few books, a desk, and a light. It may be that you bring into that space every sacred thing that you have to inspire you: diplomas from your university; pictures of your family; a thesaurus, a dictionary, phone numbers that you might need; or favorite pieces of writing. What you are creating is not only a nest but an altar for your creativity.

In the shamanic way of teaching and in my way of approaching the reality of writing, there is a sacredness to what you do because with your words—whether you are writing about gardening, butterflies, the process of enlightenment, or biography—you change

# The Directional Cross of the Writer's Spirit

## North
*Your experience and your vision
piercing reality like an Eagle's Eye.*
Light, inspiration, and wisdom.
Input from the universe.
The glow of your talent
translated into words.

## West
*Like a Great Bear
hibernating when
winter comes.*
The dream of your project.
Transformation of self
and readers.
Death of your dream
as you awake;
the rebirth of it
in a new form.

## Center
*Listen like a Wolf to
the wind. Scent the
direction of the many
trails of your story
and choose one.*
Spiritual metabolism.
Temple of universal life.

## East
*Like a Snake shedding
its rational skin.*
Concepts borrowed from
conditioning and society.
Old wise one who speaks
truth within you.
Trickster, sacred clown who
tests your vision and
intelligence of the heart.
Trickster lives a lie.

## South
*Like a Mouse and the creatures who have their noses
closest to the ground, you build your creative nest.*
Physical effort to focus.
Setting out your desk.
Preparing your writing altar.
Research.
Details of composition, pages,
and publishing.

people. The way you perceive the world is different from the way others perceive the world. You may already know that. Nonetheless, it lies at the very source of your self and your art, and it is sacred. You must take responsibility for it.

What you place in your sacred nest are pieces of writing that change you, that bring you to a higher place, pieces of writing that have saved your life at some time in the past, things that bring you to your sacred center.

It may take months to gather your place of writing in a way that feeds you, in a way that supports you. You want to make sure that you totally accomplish this.

As you look at the South, you also look at the research you have done. Perhaps you place it in your sacred space, perhaps not. Just make sure that you have done your homework. Pragmatic issues like composition, the number of pages, and publishing are all done in the South on the Wheel. What is the venue of publishing? For whom are you writing? Who is your audience? What are you trying to accomplish with this book? You look at the number of pages. Is it a small book? Is this a book of hundreds of pages?

Now move to the West of your Writer's Wheel. Here, you dream and think of a great bear hibernating when winter comes. It is in the West that you have the dream of your project. You should write this dream down, just as you did with your research and outline in the South. The West is the place where you as self are transformed, and therefore, your readers become transformed. It is the direction where there is a great depth of your dream and you go to sleep with it, dream with it, and wander down the trails of that dream. Then, as you wake, you realize that out of this dream is the rebirth of a new form. There you find what it is that you are really going to write. You work with this. You can visualize different aspects of your project and of your characters. Each of your characters should be dreamed on. Work with them, dream them, see where they go. What is the life of this particular character? Is it evil or of the light? Is he a manipulator? Is he ill? Where are all your characters? How do *they* interplay on the Wheel? Do you have a West character—a very dreamy, ungrounded person who needs desperately to look across the Wheel to the East and work with the mind and the Old Wise One within?

Work with the dream of your project and all of the characters within it. Work with the flow of that dream and how it looks. Is it a raging river or a stream? Is it a still pond reflecting the face of nature and the many people who are in your story?

Then you move to the North on the Wheel. The North represents light, inspiration, and wisdom. It is arrived at through your dreaming in the West and the foundation that you have settled into from the south. The North is the place where you find the glow of your talent translated. It is in the North that you find the input from the universe, from the stars, from the moon, from the sun, from the clouds and the sky. You relate these aspects to what you are doing. Your experience and your vision are piercing reality at this point like an eagle's eye. The eagle is in the North and has far-seeing vision. This becomes a very strong spiritual position. From the north you look across the Wheel to the South, the place of manifestation. Actually, the perspective of inspiration in the North married to your talent helps you to bring into clear balance all aspects of the Wheel. When you focus on spirit or divine guidance, for instance, the west, the dream of your story takes on a new depth that helps bridge your writing through heat and new vision and creates color and a fusion of emotions and higher values.

Then you move to the East. In the East are the mental aspects of your book, which balance the emotions of the West. East is the place of rationality, of the mental male, and the Old Wise One within you. The Owl, the sacred wise one, the trickster, also sits in the East. Here you find that you are like a snake shedding its rational skin. You look at the concepts that you have borrowed from the conditioning of society and the structures you have been through, and you shed what is no longer of use to you, that which no longer serves you. The Old Wise One speaks truth within you. We all have an Old Wise One, an old woman or man, something that is sacred and eternal that seems to have a way of accessing the Akashic record, the agreement that you have with your soul of everything you have done or ever will do, a library of consciousness that is available to us all. There is a trickster in the East, as well, a sacred clown who tests your vision and the intelligence of your heart. It tests all that you have set up to make sure that it is honest, that it has integrity, that it is balanced, and that it means something.

At this point, you have now gone around the Wheel. You have looked at your physical aspects in the South; you have looked at the dreams in the West; you have looked at the spirit and how that has manifested in your life in the North; you have looked at the East to test all that you have done to make sure that it is strong and filled out enough. If it is not, then you need to move around the Wheel again. From the South, perhaps you really need to look at the book as a series of chapters and headings and categories. From the West, make sure that your emotions are balanced with the East and your mind. Spirit in the North needs to be balanced with the physical in the South.

In the Center of any Wheel is the self. It is from that place of sacred self that you look at the other directions of the Wheel. In the Center is your writer's spirit. Like a wolf, you sit in the Center and listen to the wind and sniff the scent of the air for the direction of the many trails of your story. You choose one trail by looking at the different aspects around the Wheel, for that is where you find your spiritual metabolism. Just as all of the directions of the Wheel are aspects of the self—with your spirit, the most essential aspect of self, at the Center—so too are all directions of the Directional Cross of the writer's spirit aspects of your writing self, aspects of your story. Your spirit is the most essential aspect of life, and therefore it is a temple. You are a temple of universal life. All of the life-giving energy that you find in life is brought through your center and from there expressed outward in your writing.

Remember, too, that it is important to stay in good physical shape while you are writing, so you need to exercise your body. So many of the memories of this lifetime and of past lifetimes are held in the muscles in your body. For your perceptions to be complete, exercise is vastly important to help the oxygen and blood and all the different chemicals of the brain and your body to be balanced and to give forth the energy and the concepts that you need and have perhaps forgotten long ago but are held there for you to rediscover. Exercise helps you do that on a very real and important level.

One is never afraid of the unknown; one is afraid of the unknown coming to an end.    —KRISHNAMURTI

# SPIRIT DREAMING

*"Little Wolf, all curled up, are you ready to see your Dreamlodge?"* Agnes asked as she flung her parka over a nail on the wall and began setting out biscuits and tea.

*"Sure,"* I said, excited but not awake enough to say much else.

*"How are you feeling?"* Agnes asked me as we sat across from each other over lunch. Warm beacons of sunlight shone through the windows and reflected off the bundles of herbs, the drums, feathers, and rattles hanging from the rafters.

*"A little apprehensive,"* I replied.

Agnes raised her eyebrows at me and pursed her lips thoughtfully.

*"We can't change this world through war,"* she said, spooning honey onto her biscuit. *"It is time to celebrate and make our own ceremonies by dancing and singing and learning to live our dreams. But first we must know how to dream."*

I nodded my head and sipped my tea.

*"What is the first step to dreaming?"* Agnes asked.

*I thought back to our time in Australia with Ginevee and the Sacred Dreamtime. "An ability to visualize."*

*"Visualization is essential, but what is behind being able to visualize?"*

*"Being able to believe in your imagination," I replied.*

*"That's right. But remember that believing is a tricky concept. A belief structure not only limits your imagining, but also limits your entire consciousness."*

*"Would a better word be* trusting?*" I asked.*

*"Yes, trusting what comes is part of loving. It is your trust that builds the bridge between this physical dream we live in and the dream of your spirit. In a sense that is what love is made of—the totality of mind and soul. The bridge or connection, then, is trust. When you found Windhorse, your spirit-man, he came to you on a beam of trust. It was not your imagination that created him, but it was your imagination that found him and allowed him to ride across that beam of light into your heart. You never doubted his being, and so you never limited his existence."**

Throughout history and in almost every tradition—Aboriginal Australians, Zen Buddhists, Native Americans—mystics everywhere consider dreaming to be a conscious activity, not an *unconscious* activity. Some of the world's greatest art—painting, sculpture, writing, and dance—has come from dreaming. An artist goes to sleep and dreams; he visits strange and wonderful places, or maybe he visits quite boring places or places that terrify the mind. And by the time he wakes up, a new and wonderful idea or image is in the process of being born. Much of art throughout the ages has

*Lynn Andrews, *The Woman of Wyrrd: Arousal of the Inner Fire* (San Francisco: Harper & Row, 1990).

first come to the artist in dream. I talk, write, and teach a great deal about dreaming and being in the dream body. This is called lucid dreaming.

Many years ago I was in the north of Canada with Agnes Whistling Elk at her cabin. She was teaching me about dreaming, talking about preparing for dreaming and the difference between falling asleep and moving consciously into sleep, about becoming very aware of being in the dreamtime. As Agnes talked to me about dreaming, we watched elk feed and the beautiful young babies of all the wild animals scamper through the trees and sunlight, out of the rocks and into burrows, drinking from the crystal clear streams coming from the north and the glaciers of snow. We walked along the banks of the stream, chewing on jerky and talking, and Agnes would impart wisdom to me in preparation for my own journeys into the dreamtime.

When you move consciously into sleep, you develop the ability to become very aware of being in the dreamtime. I have recounted much of her ancient wisdom about spirit dreaming in my book *The Woman of Wyrrd,* and I think it merits revisiting especially here in a book about writing spirit. As a writer, I want to help *you* as a writer access your dreaming, access your ability to dream, imagine, and visualize. Agnes told me as she prepared me to move into my dream body that when you have a sense of a past life, remember that what you imagine is real. This is especially important for the writer to understand, because so much of our art is entwined with our imagination. If something can become real for me, then I can make it real in my writing. She also told me that when you have a sense of a past life, you need to find the roots of a future life to create a sense of balance. That is what we do as we develop our stories, we move our characters and our plots and our story lines from a past life toward a future life.

*Many people find books like* Lolita *or* Madame Bovary *disturbing because they upset people's notions of who they are or who they could be. Many people don't like that. And that is why all great innovations, at the start, become great disturbances. It's ony later on that we act as if they have habitually been there. But I look around me and I see a telephone or a car or an airplane. And I think, "My God! How much imagination has gone into any of these instruments?"*\*

Moving between a sense of a past life and finding the roots of a future life seems like an irrational concept except when you apply it within the concept of storytelling. It certainly is not part of our usual life flow. Humor me for a moment, even if you don't believe in it, as you stretch the boundaries of your imagination. When you go back to your writing, you will feel broader, wider, where you can envelop the corridors of a vast world that you may never have seen before but that visits you on occasion with ideas, knocking at your consciousness, wanting to be heard, wanting you to tell the story it has to give you. From this moment forward it is my urgent desire that you will consider dreaming as a totally conscious act and that you will become fully lucid not only in your dreaming but in your living as well.

One of the first things that you do to facilitate the process of lucid dreaming is to find your hands or feet or something very familiar to you in your sleep. Make a conscious effort to see your hands or your feet as you begin to slip into the dreamtime; find them and as you go along, hold your attention on them. As you develop more facility with this, you can find things that someone has hidden, say in a drawer. You find these things, look at them, and learn to keep your attention on them. While sleeping, the

---

\*Azar Nafisi, *Reading Lolita in Tehran* (New York: Random House, 2003).

ability to keep your attention focused and not move from one place to another is very important, because you are beginning to form a dream body, a sacred will, which you will use from now on when you are in the dreamtime. Always remember, if you do not like where you are in a dream, you can change the dream, and you don't have to wake up to do so. This may sound farfetched, but it really is not.

As a writer, you might become very interested in finding and speaking with the ancient masters. Although this may sound incredible, wouldn't you love to avail yourself of great writers, of Shakespeare even, or of great periods of history where the men and women of high degree searched for truth? To avail yourself of how they found it? These things are important to us as writers because we don't want to write words that just splash across the page in a very superficial way. Deep attracts deep throughout one's lifetime. As you go deeper into the soul, to that place within you where writing occurs, you can actually find the means to access the masters of creativity, access the masters of dreaming. What fun! Your writing is a bridge between who you are now and who you can become as a writer, what you can produce in the world and how you can become recognized. Isn't that something that sounds like a place of enjoyment for you?

One of the things I want to help you develop is the ability to listen to your body and understand the power and the incredible life force that is running through you. You store power in your body. Begin to notice your feelings, your sensations, how your energy is moving. Your body has a wisdom. You begin to become conscious of the wisdom and what drives your body, what your body feels like at different times of the day. What does it feel like in the morning? What does it feel like when you are with people? If you ignore the signals your body sends to you, you will begin to dissipate your power and begin to destroy your body through stress, because you are not paying attention to who you really are. Recognize that the Great Spirit has given you an extraordinary gift. That gift is life force. We can't explain life force. Nobody can. But we can begin to understand it by listening to the body and remembering that the body is an ally. The ally is a source of wisdom that will appear in your visualizations. It can also appear through your body. This happens through sensations. As an example, perhaps you are walking through the deserts of the American Southwest with all of the exotic cactus and sage and the abundance of other strange and beautiful plant life that grows in parts of those deserts. You look around and your vision is limitless as you look over this vast expanse of earth that is the desert unbounded. And you have the feeling that nature is immense. You realize that there is so much truth in beauty, that beauty indeed is truth and truth is visible in nature.

Sometimes when your body hurts, it is the ally that is trying to be heard. You ask yourself, what drives your body? What or who is it inside you that is trying to move you, for example, through your fatigue and exhaustion? When you have a sense of this, where is it coming from? From your solar plexus? From your mind? From your heart or your back?

Your body can store power. We let go of that power when we don't love our bodies and stop trusting them. Your body has saved you through its instinct many times, for example when you leaped out of the way of an oncoming car that you didn't even know was there. As you spend more and more time being conscious about the way you move, you begin to find your own authenticity, your own truth. For example, perhaps you find that you are walking hunched over, and as you continue the movement of walking, you realize that you have closed your heart chakra, the ability to love and express emotion. Maybe you find yourself trying to walk in a position that eases your back, and you realize perhaps that in life you are backing away from your power. Or perhaps your knees are sore because you have trouble moving forward in life. You begin to find what is authentic for you and make the changes you need to make.

In every way, dreaming is about being authentic, and dream body work is about allowing your body to speak to you. In his book *Dreaming While Awake*, psychologist Arnold Mindell writes that the body is an extraordinary antenna. If you have created your dream body—as the Sisterhood of the Shields and I and most of the masters with whom I have worked have—it becomes important to listen to the body and remember that the body is an ally, a source of the wisdom that will appear in your writing and in your visualization. In every way, dreaming is about being authentic. We so often don't stay in touch with who we are or what we came into this lifetime to learn. And when we move off this path, we move off our truth. Mindell recounts the following story about his experiences in Australia with an Aboriginal elder:

> *Uncle Lewis Obrien, an Aboriginal elder with whom we were walking, gently put his hand on my shoulder and said quietly, "Arny, look over there, in the direction of the center of the city. What do you see?" I told him that I saw Victoria Square, the noisy bustling business center of the city. Hundreds of people were shopping, cars honked and buses moved slowly through traffic.*
>
> *"Looks like a busy city," I said.*
>
> *Uncle Lewis suggested that I take another look. When I looked again, all I saw was the same noisy city.*
>
> *"Well, your sight is good, but you don't see the Dreaming. White fellas don't see the Dreaming. But they sense it anyhow. White fellas built the center of the city there. We Aboriginal people used to camp where the center is now; that's where the Dreaming is*

strongest. Victoria Square is a wonderful place; that's why the modern business works so well over there."

My environmental consciousness was both shocked and enlightened. I realized how my view of the city was filtered through the lens of my U.S. background and education. Until meeting this elder, given the choice I tended to avoid cities, preferring the countryside. Uncle Lewis made me realize that the miracle of nature I was looking for in the countryside was right in front of me, in the midst of the bustling city. The Dreaming is always present, like an aura shimmering around the objects and events we call everyday life.

Some Aboriginal peoples describe the Dreaming in terms of the dark side of the moon. When the moon is not quite full, you see its bright, illuminated side. You might call it a half moon. But if you look closely on a clear evening, you can see the dark side, silently shimmering next to the more apparent bright side. Like me, most people focus only on the bright side of the moon and ignore the dark face, that is, the Dreaming reality.

The bright side is only that portion of the whole moon that is illuminated. Focusing only on the bright side of the moon and ignoring the dark side might easily make you think that the dark side does not exist, while in fact we need the dark side to represent the whole moon.

The same is true for everything you see. If you only focus on everyday reality, you neglect the Dreaming. According to Aboriginal thinking, the Dreaming is the basic substance of the material world. The Dreaming gives objects the energy that attracts and repels your attention. If you neglect the Dreaming, you devalue the material environment because you ignore its basis and thus miss half of life.

The power of Dreaming is right here, behind the everyday world, as part of every object, the part you sometimes forget to notice. From the Aboriginal perspective, everyday reality is the bright side of the moon pointing to the power of Dreaming, the moon's dark side.

# Spirit Dreaming

*. . . Without Dreaming, nothing would exist. Dreaming is the energy behind everything; it is the life force of all living beings, the power of trees and plants, and the power of motors, business, and financial centers.*

*An artist senses the Dreaming in the canvas, paper and stone and knows that everyday reality is not only concrete. Leonardo da Vinci wrote that artists should look into the peeling plaster walls until they can see images emerging from the shapes of the plaster. Similarly, Michelangelo called sculpting a process of bringing out the form that already exists inside the stone. Artists and Aboriginal peoples have developed the ability to see the Dreaming, that is, the power behind the figures you see in your nighttime dreams and everyday reality.* \*

In short, you need to focus on your dreaming every bit as much as you do on your everyday reality. Out of dreams come great stories. Lucid dreaming is a way to attract these stories to you, instead of waiting to see if any will come to you. Consider Agnes's speaking in my *Woman of Wyrrd*.

*"We have spoken together of doubling. Doubling occurs in the physical."*

*"You mean when you are in one place and you can appear physically in another place at the same time."*

*"That is approximately what it means," Agnes said. "There is no way to explain these things in a rational language, because they are, again, part of the shadow world, part of the unknowable. But as closely as I can explain it to you in words, you could be here—and if your intent and your spirit intention were strong enough—you would*

---

\*Arnold Mindell, *Dreaming While Awake* (Charlottesville, VA: Hampton Roads Publishing Company, Inc., 2000).

be able to be here physically with me and still manifest the form of your body somewhere else. It would not be your physical body, but someone could see you and think it was your physical body. Now what you're doing in the Dreamlodge here is different," she said.

I closed the flap to the Dreamlodge and went back to sit near Agnes, next to the fire. "What do you call what I'm doing?" I asked.

"It is called doubling in the Dreamtime, or dream-walking. You are not exactly just dreaming. You are actually sending your consciousness into a separate time, so that you are not moving in the astral but beyond it. You must remember that when you move out of this physical, dualistic existence, you are moving away from the reference of the time-space relativity that we experience here." Agnes patted the floor of the Dreamlodge with the palms of her hands. "We are moving out of time. That is why when you are working in the astral, it is impossible to tell what time it is. What you are doing when you dream-walk, Lynn, is moving into history, into the past. You are exploring your lifeline. When you leave your body, you are going down your cord, which has existed through your many lifetimes and has been created by your spirit connection with the Great Spirit."

"You mean to tell me that there is an actual cord that leads from each of my lives to the next?"

"Yes, my daughter, it leads from one lifetime to another until it goes full circle. It isn't going from beginning to end but full circle."

"Then do we just go on forever in that circle, reliving our lives?"

"You don't exactly relive your lives. You become a dreamwalker. Physical existence is structured to teach you things through the possibility of mirrors. You create your mirrors during a physical existence in this body that you are: you gather a family; you gather a husband, friends, a teacher like myself. And you learn from us. You learn from the reflection that you see. We are mirrors for you. You chose us. You learn as much as you're capable of learning. You have *all that you need in this lifetime to become enlightened; whether that happens or not is really up to you."*

*"Everyone has the chance to become enlightened in one lifetime?" I asked.*

*"Yes, everyone has that opportunity. Everyone has what he or she needs, the mirrors. Each of us has asked, before being born, for everything needed. The problem is, when we are born, we become caught in the dream. We are born into a kind of sleep. To become enlightened is to wake up from that dream. . . ."**

---

*Lynn Andrews, *Woman of Wyrrd: The Arousal of the Inner Fire* (San Francisco: Harper & Row, 1990).

The dividing line between good and evil passes, not between the other and me, but right down the middle of my forehead, between my left side and my right.   —LANZO DEL VASTO

# PERCEPTION

If you change the way you perceive something, then what you are looking at changes. It is the same way with your writing. You may look at your writing and find you want to make a shift in it; you don't know quite what you mean by that, only that you feel there has to be a new dimension added, a new perspective. I would suggest at this point that to create that new perspective, you have to change the way you are looking at what you are writing. One of the ways that you do this is by moving into a place of silence, a place of *true* silence, in order to develop a new sense of communion with your work.

When there is that silence in your being, it means that your "roof chatter," that constant inner dialogue, is finally stopped and you experience total emptiness. All the clamor of the conscious mind trying to get your attention finally ceases. At this point, facts usually begin to move through your mind. If you sit in silence and watch these thoughts come and go, you will likely find that it becomes a process of the conscious mind trying to vie for your attention. Idea follows idea until you find yourself back in the midst of the roof chatter, and now it is fear that catches your attention: How am I going to make a living if I just sit here in silence trying to find emptiness, not doing anything? Sitting in silence feels like meditation, like you are not doing anything concrete. You need always to be doing something concrete because otherwise you are going to starve to death.

But if you are sincere enough in your search for the ability to become silent, then suddenly somewhere along this trail a flood comes through, a flood of silence. It is in this flood of silence that all of the psychic debris, all of the baggage that you have collected in your lifetime, in your process of writing, is simply flooded away and an emptiness actually happens.

Then a kind of truth comes. And it is in this truth, found through these moments of emptiness and silence, that perhaps the first glimpses of your writing—the real proof of your writing, the essence of your writing—begin to happen. All of a sudden the barriers disappear and your creative eyes are open, perhaps for the first time. It is the most astounding, powerful experience. And you realize how much of your writing, how much of the subject you are approaching, is being missed. Maybe you have been seeing it only from one aspect, from emotion in the West or spirit in the North. You haven't explored the intellect in the East or the physical realm of your subject in the South. You have not experienced the totality of your writing process, perhaps, until now.

It's not easy to move into moments of silence where the emptiness really happens. It may leave you with a feeling of letting go, of releasing control. We are all control freaks, for the most part. We don't want to be damaged. We don't want to be used. We don't want to be hurt. So we hold on to control of things. But when you hold control of the creative process, it is almost impossible to be creative, to express yourself truthfully. It is also very, very difficult for impulse to come in, for those moments of epiphany, of vision, to get through. And you miss something. It is sitting in the silence and letting go of absolutely everything, including what you think is true, letting all of it go, that realization comes and you begin to see truly the evolution of your thought patterns. Those thought patterns do not come from the mind. They come from your heart and soul.

Remember that the mind has had to be conditioned to become the great instrument that it is, but it can usher into existence only that which has already been put into it. What is coming from your inspiration is coming from the epiphanies of Spirit, the creative God-force or whoever you would like to label it. I don't ask you to believe in anything, but I ask you to believe in your own ability to be an instrument who is so evolved that inspiration can come in from other levels of existence, from creativity and higher consciousness.

Here's an exercise you can do to experience this level of epiphany. Sit in silence in an ennobling place, on a ridge or a foothill somewhere in a deserted area of a park, or at an altar that you've built in your home, which might be pages and pages of your writing. Light a candle or create any form of a ceremony that consecrates your surroundings for a moment. And use this ceremony as a gateway for expression to come through to you. Perhaps an ancestor of yours will express herself to you. But remain in silence. Expect anything and expect nothing! Expect yourself to drain out your mind, your self, finally. Allow that flood of silence to happen so that something new, something you never thought of, can come in. Maybe what comes in is only the sound of the beat of your heart, but remember that manifestation *comes* between the beats of the heart.

And then get to the point where you listen to nothing, again. All of a sudden this emptiness makes you realize that your perceptions have been clouded. Clouded with what? Clouded with mental activity, with thoughts, with memories, with ideas that keep you from the very thing that you are trying to find, which is your image of truth, the essence of you that is greatness. Everyone has an image of greatness. Some people have better access to it than others. Allow yourself to feel your image of greatness and witness it as you sit in a comfortable position, not in a position that is difficult to get into. Wherever you are, be comfortable so that you can forget about your body for a while. Move into the silence, into the shadows of the trees, into a new person within you and allow it to express something new.

At first, as an initiate, you are trying to go from what you believe to be real into the dream. In taking this very, very great step in your life, you are going from what you have dreamed of and hoped to be possible into making it an actuality in the written word. That is why you start to feel the responsibility of becoming a writer deeply within you. Your dreams and your hopes are becoming a great reality. Like others, you have not been truly contented with yourself as you are. You've been constantly in a state of shifting sands and discontent. Writing becomes the possibility of transcending all that. As a writer, you have always known that whoever you have been is not your real and true being. You feel as if you're wearing a series of masks, each one a mask that you can put on and then take off. You have always been looking for your own expression as a writer. But you're never quite sure how you'd look without a mask. And writing, your writing is the mirror. In your search for your real essence, you cannot become contented with the mask that society has given you. You realize that your creative life is the only thing that is truly worthwhile for you. You are a rainbow. You carry all the spectrum of colors, nuances, textures, and light within you. You are becoming capable of living that essence, the rainbow you are as a creative person.

In my work, I talk a great deal about butterflies, especially Butterfly Woman, who is exclusively atop the Butterfly Tree in *Jaguar Woman*. I have always seen people as being like caterpillars. Yet we see and think of ourselves as imprisoned in a cocoon instead of simply being in a stage of growth. We don't see that it's just a passing phase of life to be in that cocoon. We don't realize that we actually have wings and that we can fly, that we can reach for what we have always thought to be impossible. So as writers what is most important is to see ourselves as a caterpillar in a cocoon and sense somehow that even in this cocoon something is occurring, an evolution is happening. We are growing wings and transforming into a completely different being. As that caterpillar, we don't believe that we can fly. We just sense that something is going to happen and we are going to change.

You don't have any wings; how could you possibly fly? You ask yourself, "How can I write this book, this magazine article, this essay? How can I possibly surpass myself and become a writer, a true writer?" Someone once said, "The greatest misfortune that can happen to a man is to forget that you must surpass yourself. Man has to know that he can surpass himself. And that will be the greatest calamity for humanity, if man forgets he is not the goal, but a bridge, that he is *really* Man if he surpasses himself!"

You are learning to fly. And it is agony in so many ways, growing pains in so many ways. There is a great agony in becoming the bridge, in becoming a butterfly. But you have a great being, a great feeling within yourself, a great desire to transcend into that butterfly. We as human beings are caterpillars. That's how I see us. And as human beings, we have many different paths that we walk.

As writers, we are walking toward what we have always thought in our minds as something out of reach, something that is impossible. But in fact, as you write, as you begin growing wings, transcending, you begin to realize that your accomplishment is really in the process of transcending. It is a process. It is growth. You are coming out of the cocoon that decides you are not the impossible. A caterpillar regarded simply as a worm cannot possibly fly to the top of the tree. But when a seed is planted in the earth, there is a shell to that seed and eventually, through warm moisture and the process of DNA, through the process of evolving, of genetics, the tree bursts through the seed and becomes something completely different from what was encased in the seed. This is the caterpillar evolving from within the cocoon.

In my book *Jaguar Woman,* I spoke about being reborn, about flying up the Butterfly Tree to the inspiration at the top. That is your book. That is your writing. That is your inspiration.

Ocean wind through emerald clouds.
Night islets and the moon bright.
After one good line, stop.
A great river spreads across your path.

—Sikong Tu (837–908)

20

# PATIENCE

Patience is an important aspect of writing, as it is for any act of creativity. Patience is definitely something that I have always had to learn. It is a quality that so many people today lack and they miss so very much. There is a wonderful story about Buddha that relates to what I want to share with you.

Buddha and his apprentice were walking along a trail. They passed a beautiful, clear pond reflecting the clouds above. They walked on several miles until they reached a village. There they sat under a tree, meditating. Buddha looked over at his apprentice and asked him to go back to the pond.

The apprentice remembered that they had seen bullocks pulling wagons going to that pond to water. The apprentice knew that the pond would be muddy, full of leaves and undrinkable. He mentioned that to Buddha. But Buddha said, "No, go to that pond."

The apprentice again said, "But if I go to the river, it won't be as dirty. It will be better water."

But Buddha was insistent. "No. Go to the pond that we passed."

Because Buddha was his master, the apprentice went, grumbling all the way. When he got to the pond some time had passed. During that period of time, the bullocks had left and the pond had a chance to settle down and clear so that by the time the apprentice got there, the water was sparkling pure again, reflecting the clouds above. The apprentice realized, "What a magnificent teaching!" He put water in the bucket and walked back to Buddha. When he saw Buddha, he said, "Thank you for the beautiful lesson you have given me. Patience is the lesson. What a wonderful way of teaching! What a wonderful thing! I now see that I must have patience and the water will clear."

Buddha looked at his apprentice and said, "Yes, we are so busy that we don't take the time to sit and dream and allow our minds to settle. So I tell you, dear apprentice, to sit beside your mind and allow your mind to still. Allow your thoughts to float away. Allow yourself to simply settle like the mud that has been stirred from the bottom of the pond. Let it settle back down until, finally, your thoughts and your ideas become crystal clear. It is then that your writing can begin."

As a writer, allow yourself to find the clarity and the purity that you would see in a pond after it has had a chance to settle.

You must do the thing you think you cannot do.

—Eleanor Roosevelt

## INTENSITY

How in the world do we handle our need to have intensity enter our world and our work? As a mystic, I would explain it this way. I would say the beginning of your work as a writer is like walking along through the low country, the valleys, enjoying the rivers and looking at the mountains above, not ever dreaming that you might reach the summit of those mountains. Then, one day, you begin to write and you begin to climb. Every day you meet a new challenge that may reflect aspects of your talent you never knew truly existed. You keep hiking toward the summit, never really thinking you might actually arrive. Your need for intensity—your need to get to the top—increases.

Near the middle of your book, you feel a shift downward in your intensity, maybe even a complete washout, and you take a day for rest. That day turns into three, and then maybe a week. And then a whole new dimension as a writer emerges: You wonder where this is going to lead. When you read back over what you have done, you may even question whether it is any good at all and whether you should continue. You ask yourself, "How can I make this beautiful?" You have reached a plateau. All I can say to you is that we all feel like this at different times. Usually around halfway through a work, we drop the momentum. Perhaps you've been working all summer, and suddenly it's fall. It is now a different season.

This is a critical moment.

At this time you need to look at your work and ask yourself: Am I being completely honest? Am I authentic? What is it that I am really trying to say in these pages? The answers you thought at the beginning of your work may be quite different now. As we have discussed before, all stories have a life of their own, and yours may have gone a different way than you expected.

You may find that it is the fool who has been writing, the clown. The sacred clown, the fool, is always in a position of power because it lives in the place of humor. The sacred clown tests the existing situations, social mores, and ceremonies to see if in fact they are real and true. With the pueblo Native Americans, there is the *koshari* who is striped horizontally. The *koshari* eats watermelon, pees on the sacred altar, fornicates, and does everything he can think of to test the validity of the belief structures, the feelings, and the ambitions. In a sense, you need to be a *koshari* when you look at your writing. You need to look at it with humor, not comparison. You need to look at it with discernment, with an eye toward what your own striving for perfection is. Comparison is a killer. You are unlike anyone who has ever lived, and you will create something that is unlike anything that has ever been done. Know that and be secure in it. Be secure in your instability and know that instability is a gift.

Vulnerability, too, is a great gift. For instance, if you are a warrior or a martial artist, you draw a circle in the sand and you stand in the center of that circle. That is your boundary. You know the truth of that boundary, and if anyone advances across that boundary, you have the right to do whatever is necessary to get that person out of your circle of power. If someone wants to enter your circle, push against you, you must have a vulnerability, an emptiness, so that when they push against you, they push against nothing. They push right through you. They can't find you, not because you are not secure in your truth but because you don't have ego about your truth. You know who you are, and you don't have to prove anything. You just simply sit in the center of your beingness, and you write. From that place of power, you are invincible.

As you look at all that you have created, try to be the mystic, the warrior or the warrioress for a moment. See that your writing creates a circle, a circle that expresses your truth in some way. That is why I gave you the Sacred Wheel. You can test your writing. Is it physically truthful as you have written it? Is it emotionally truthful? Do you express your dream? Is there a thought in your writing about life, death, transformation, and rebirth in some way? It can be very subtle, remember. Go to the North. Does your work balance the inspiration of your ideas with the presentation of those ideas and spirit? Presentation is in the South; inspiration is in the North. Do they balance each other? Have you had an epiphany so profound that you feel as if you should write the Bible? Or you may have had no epiphany at all—you simply wanted to write a really fun mystery story or romance. There is still an inspiration to begin. There is an inspiration to want to create something. That to me is an epiphany of its own. That epiphany should balance with the manifestation of your concepts.

Now go to the East and look at how you have rationally projected the whole story. Is it understandable physically? Are you moving along a story line in a way that translates to someone who may never have thought of these ideas, doesn't know the patterns of experiences that you are expressing? Does it balance with the emotion in the West? In the West, emotion should balance the mind in the East and vice versa. Also in the East is the Old Wise One, the one who tells you if there is something missing. Listen to the voice of the Old Wise One. See if you agree or not.

Of course, in the South you are physically dealing with the challenges of creating your masterpiece, because for you, no matter what kind of writing it is, it is indeed a masterpiece. You as the writer are the hero. You have gone into an unknown land to learn, to teach, to write, to talk about the unknown. And you bring back the treasure of that experience to other people. Not only do you bring it back in the last part of your book, but you are also going to present the treasure and share it with people. Your characters are going to do that. You, as a writer, are going to do that with your readers.

This is what occurs for all of us around the middle of our book. We look at the momentum. We look at the summit of the mountain that we are climbing, wondering if ever we will attain that height. And then we go for it. We write the last part of our book with a different kind of energy from what we had in the beginning. We respect it and we respect ourselves for being able to find spiritual endurance. It takes a great deal of endurance to write the beginning, middle, and end of a story.

If the term spiritual endurance irritates you, look at it again. When I say spiritual, I am talking about the balance of all of life, of all of nature. I don't talk about religion. I talk about the ability for people of high degree, as they would say in Australia, to be able to choreograph the energies of the universe and the energies of writing. How do you choreograph light and texture and art and extraordinary adventure and mystery into what you write, into what you do in the world? As one wonderful scriptwriter in Hollywood once told me, "Lynn, if you are going to write a script, you show things in actions, not in words like you do in a book." He told me about one scene that he had just written. He talked about a woman and a man entering an elevator. You could tell instantly by the action that the man was very attracted to the woman and felt her presence. He smoothed his hair. He adjusted his tie. He was subtly watching her out of his peripheral vision. She also was aware of him. She dropped something onto the floor of the elevator on purpose. The man instantly picked it up and gave it to her. Nothing was spoken in this scene, but he took the handkerchief she had dropped and very subtly sniffed it before returning it to her, leaving no question in the audience's mind that an energy was going on between them. In a sense, something very akin to power is in that scene.

You are in a very joyous mood and somebody says to you, "Why are you so happy?" If you start thinking about it, you will probably drop out of the joyous mood almost immediately: "Well, it's because I got a raise. Well, I don't know, I just feel happy." If someone asks you to describe power, you can talk around the subject. You can describe the effect of power and what it is not, but if you describe power directly, you will lose the power and it will no longer be there. There is no way to explain the unexplainable.

Now at the middle of your book, you look back over what you have documented, what you have done, what you have described and see if there is a more economical way to use your words. I would only use words that you truly need, as Hemingway described. Use what is necessary to express a feeling, a scene, a situation. But first you need to get the bones, the structure, the armature down onto paper before you begin to delete or add words to what you already have. Once you get the feeling of the overall book, the first draft, then you go back over it and feel the energy from one end to the other. You feel the ebb and flow of the chapters. At the middle, it is the beginning of that recapitulation of what you have divined on paper. Enjoy it.

The most difficult climb is ahead of you. You are more tired, yet you are more inspired, perhaps, than you were at the beginning. As you begin to look toward the sky, toward the summit of the Mount Everest that you have created for yourself, as you begin to climb on a more vertical stretch, the mountain, the book, is asking you what you are made of. Can you do it really? Can you climb me? Now the book, although you think you have created this story, is really re-creating you.

There is no question that when you begin a work of art, you begin a process of remembering and also of forgetting. This is a wonderful teaching. At some point near the middle of the book, you forget who you were when you began the book. You probably have forgotten who you were when you began your entire journey of writing exploration, but you remember, finally, not only who you are going to become and who you have become, but why you really were born in the first place and what you chose, in actuality, to learn in this life. What you chose to write about, you probably chose longer ago than you can remember.

I have no parents—I make the heavens and earth my parents. I have no home—I make awareness my home.

—Samurai, fourteenth century

# SHAPE-SHIFTING

Shape-shifting. What do you think that means? You might think that it is a term used only by anthropologists or shamans, not in the real world but only in the world of mystery. But in fact we are a thought form. We create through our ability to conceptualize. We create our bodies and who we are as a lifestyle and a life-form and a dream body. Shape-shifting in writing is the same. You are a person sitting in Iowa with this incredible dream that you have of a novel, a book, or a concept, and suddenly you shape-shift from a person tending her garden and making a living in some very unrelated way into a wonderful writer.

I do not believe that shape-shifting is an ancient term that cannot be applied to our own lives. When you are walking down a trail and you see something magnificent up in a tree, perhaps an eagle high in flight, you shape-shift in a way out of old negative paradigms into someone who is grateful for your eyes, for the ability to see, for the incredible presence of life in all its forms.

When you write, the same thing happens; you are moving along with an idea that you have, maybe you've wandered off track a little and are becoming frustrated with your story, and all of a sudden you have a new insight, a surge of inspiration that takes you to a whole new level of consciousness as an individual and within your writing. You have just shape-shifted yourself and your story!

As a writer and as a teacher, I want to penetrate into alternative possibilities for our own perceptions and awareness in life. I do not want to submerge you in any kind of confusion. I want, rather, to bring you to a different way of seeing the reality of your state in life and your health, basically give you a road map. I want to shake things up a little within you so that you begin to see that life in this the world is rooted in a much more mysterious paradigm than you ever realized.

There are two aspects of life: what southern sorcerers and shamans call the *Tonal,* which is the everyday physical life, and the *Nagual,* which is your life of spirit. In the way of the Sisterhood of the Shields, I use a little different terminology. I say that we live in the ordinary world of first attention, the physical, and as we become more aware, we move into a parallel reality that I call second attention, dreaming, the dreaming process. All of the work that I do with the dream body, for instance, is done with a foot secure in the physical because you never leave the body; it just appears so as you move into the parallel reality of spirit. Another attention, which is spoken of less frequently, is third attention, the ability to perceive even higher levels of consciousness while choreographing the dance between first and second attentions.

Shape-shifting is an extraordinary event in the way that most people think. Some years ago I was in the Yucatán with Zoila and José, Zoila being one of the women in the Sisterhood of the Shields and an extraordinary teacher. We were all sitting around in a hut in the jungle. One night we had done ceremony, and we were talking, sharing stories, and doing wonderful things together in the most simple ways. One of the women was mending a sandal; another was working on a mask. There was a fire, as it had been a little cooler that evening.

All of a sudden Zoila stood up and began to gather her energy. I could see her centering herself. All of a sudden she began to circle around the fire, circling the fire sunwise. Suddenly she turned to look at each of us in the eyes, and she took on the shape of a jaguar, which is her power animal. She snarled a wild scream and looked at us as if we were prey, then she bounded around the fire and then leaped out of the hut, leaving us absolutely spellbound. It was a spectacular example of someone shape-shifting, and I was stunned. I sat there and could not move. After a while we began to chatter again. Zoila was gone for several hours, but the next time we saw her, she was back in her human form. We could see on the earthen floor, however, marks of the jaguar where she had been circling the fire. She came back and sat down with us hours later as if nothing had occurred.

Then she began to talk about shape-shifting with Agnes, Ruby, me, and two other people who were also there. Earlier I had told her about a woman with whom I had been working who was suffering from heart disease, and apparently Zoila had been thinking about this story because she turned to me, and she couldn't imagine why this particular woman continued to suffer from heart disease the way she did. Zoila said, "Why in the world would anyone choose that dream to live in? Why would you not choose the dream of health? I cannot imagine why your people, who come down to teach us about your world, actually have so little to teach us. We have so much to teach you."

Then she said, "Don't you understand that you don't have to

choose a dream of suffering or war? You can choose a dream of well-being. You can choose a dream of success. You can choose a dream of health. Why would you do otherwise? I am healthy. Why isn't everybody else healthy?"

As the discussion progressed, I told her about a friend of mine who had cancer, who had come to me and told me that all the women in her family always got cancer around the age of forty. This friend said she was afraid that she was going to get cancer "because all of the women in her family do." And I told her to listen to what she had just said to herself. Her response was, "Well, there's nothing that I can do about it. It's not my fault and I can't help it. It's just the way my family history is." I tried to tell her that there was no fault involved, that the earth is a schoolhouse. We come here to learn; we come here to understand and to change the archaeology of our soul. In modern terms, if we have inherited the ability to have a disease and the climate in which the disease can grow, and that disease does indeed begin to grow, it means that somewhere along the line we have also picked up an attitude or a belief structure about that disease. And because we buy into that belief structure, the cellular weakness within us becomes an actual physical weakness and the beliefs we have carried about it ultimately produce exactly what it is we have feared is going to happen.

Agnes, Ruby, and the women of the Sisterhood of the Shields are dumbstruck by our human condition because we choose to allow ourselves to live in a state of consciousness wherein the diseases and difficulties in our lives have a chance to grow and to prosper. If we change our attitude toward disease and change our belief structure about it, we may still be fragile in that area of our cellular structure but now we have put ourselves in a position to do something about it. We have suddenly shape-shifted from a person who is vulnerable to cancer, for example, to a person who chooses health and wellness! And it is the same with our writing. Are you someone who believes in the quiet recesses of your mind that you don't really have the possibility of becoming a good writer, of getting yourself published because we create in a climate that is not particularly supportive? If you are, you want to shape-shift out of that belief structure right now!

My friend who had cancer became very upset with me when I tried to talk with her about healing the way she was thinking because the way she was thinking was creating her physical being. She said that absolutely she was going to come down with cancer, and P.S., she did. As I was telling this to Zoila, I saw that it was as if my friend was hanging onto that concept of her health and disease like an old friend. That is why I want to shake things up a little within you as a writer *and* as a human being. What belief structures are you holding onto that are keeping you from being everything you ever wanted to be and more? Shape-shift yourself out of them, right now!

Shape-shifting comes from the heart, not the mind, especially when you are speaking about your physical and spiritual health and when you are speaking about your writing health. With the expression of your heart and your feeling, envision what you want. You want to have better health! You want to be a successful writer! This is your heartfelt dream, so why then are you living out a dream in which you are ill, in which your writing is not all you ever wanted it to be?

When I was talking about my friend with Zoila, I told her that I believe we come here to heal ourselves in this earth walk. It is not a place where we come just to be happy. We come to be fulfilled and to learn and to become whole, to become enlightened if we're very lucky. Zoila said, "Yes, that's exactly what I am talking about. Your wording is simply different." Then she scratched herself on her hand with a knife until it bled. I asked her, "Why did you do that?"

And she said, "I want you to see that tomorrow it will heal. My body heals itself without even thinking about it. That is the kind of shape-shifting I'd like you to look at because then, when you work with your people, you can talk about not only changing the way they think but also changing the energy." She said that when someone has cut himself, there is a certain energy that happens of which he is totally unconscious, but the healing energy takes place because the body knows. She told me that the important thing to see is that when she turns into a jaguar, she is a jaguar; she is shape-shifting into the oneness that all of life represents.

"But," I said, "the oneness still has separation."

Zoila said, "No, it does not have separation. Separation is our agreement in this life so that we may learn a new and different reality of oneness." She picked up a tortilla, rolled it around in some cheese, and took a big bite. Then she said, "I am at one with all of life. I can shape-shift because I know the experience of oneness, down into the core of my being. Things do not just happen to us. Shape-shifting jaguar did not just come upon me. I came upon it because I am it. You must understand, Lynn, that when you have put on masks in the past and you have written about it, oftentimes you become that mask. You become that mask because you are a part of the energy that mask creates. It is not an energy that you live every day all the time but, it is still a part of you even though you are not conscious of it."

"So what you are trying to say," I said to Zoila, "is that we have to look at our energy from a cellular level, on a personal level and on a spiritual level. And when we realize that all those energies are the same emanation of strength and power, then we realize that we can shape-shift among them."

"Exactly," Zoila said. "For instance, I took you into the jungle a few years ago and we came upon a canyon deep into the earth called *La Caldera,* and I insisted that you walk down there with me. You were terrified, Lynn, because you're afraid of heights and you saw this little, tiny trail that I wanted you to walk down. And it terrified you to the point that you were not going to follow me. I told you that if you did not follow me, none of the Sisterhood would ever work with you again. It was your time to shape-shift out of terror into a kind of trust. I knew what I was doing in asking you to follow me, but I also knew that it was time for you to move out of a fear of death and into a new level of consciousness where you could give over to your teacher completely. It was time for you to move into a place of service to higher wisdom. So, I progressed down the narrow trail and disappeared out of sight. In order for you to have followed me down the trail that day, you had to shape-shift into a complete warrior self. And you did. You moved down the trail with me. You worked through your terror. You gave up your complete addiction to the fear of death and moved into a place that you told me later was a place of trust."

It wasn't a matter of life or death; it was about trusting that I am in service. I, Lynn Andrews, am in service to the Great Spirit and whatever Great Spirit wants from me, I am here to produce it: whether it is my courage, my ability to work with people, my ability to trust and give over completely to my teachers at that point. At that point above the canyon with Zoila, I had shape-shifted, and that, Zoila said, was the beginning of my ability to learn the true nature of shape-shifting. "Someone who has a disease," she said, "has to know so totally this concept that they can shape-shift out of a place of unworthiness, a place where they have not allowed themselves to win, whatever that means in their life. They need to learn to shape-shift out of the concept of illness to a place of total well-being and health. It is a lot to ask of someone because by the nature of things we are imperfect beings and we come here to learn."

That's what this is all about. We come here to learn, little by little, how to become a total human being, free from the kind of ideas and imperfections that bring us to a place of suffering and dis-ease. As a writer, it is so important for you to understand and grasp this concept.

Everything we agree upon has been made out of energy. Therefore, our thought forms have given form to our energy body and to our physical body. That is shape-shifting. If you suddenly see the light and see what you have been doing to yourself, what you have been doing to your writing, you will see that you have supported whatever weakness you are carrying, as with the way my friend had supported her cancer through her thoughts. If you see Mother Earth as a cruel body of trees and animals that are beasts that can hurt you, stones that you have to kick out of the way so you don't trip, then you will probably have difficulty in your life. It is important to see that life can be the dream that we want it to be, not only for our personal health but also for the world. This is extremely important for us as writers to grasp. Our world has the possibility of moving out of a time of conflict into a time of love and the exchange and celebration of differences, not the hatred of difference. We have the opportunity now to shift the world out of the system of war, "In the name of God I kill you," and into something new and much better: "In the name of God I love you." To change the dream, we have to impact one another in our lives and with our writing. Use your beauty and your light and your vision.

Discover your own power or intent to make your dream become a reality. How are you going to do this, and are you prepared to be well and whole? Do you feel worthy of perfection? How are you going to find the energy to transform yourself? Energy is built partly through your imagination so that you can discover what you are holding that keeps you from healing or creating your work of art, that keeps you from succeeding. What is the energy knot that holds you separate from the healing elements that surround you, like the "holy wind"? Feel this "holy wind" caress your cheeks, the flutter of wings and feathers from a ceremonial fan, the fragrance of juniper and sage of a sacred fire. Feel the power of natural balance in the weather, the stones and waters of Mother Earth. Allow the elements to wash you clean of your restrictions, fears, and pain. Experience the joy of lifting out of confusion and doubt into a simple bliss of freedom.

Like the women in the Sisterhood, you begin to walk quietly, not staring at the trail in front of you but walking with your head up, looking at the light in the trees, looking at all of nature that surrounds you. Look at the magnificent architecture of the buildings around you, of the amazing possibilities that have been brought to fruition simply because someone refused to accept the old paradigm. Just look at modern-day flight! Don't keep your head down so that all of this wonder passes you by.

The reality of shape-shifting comes through your heart, not your mind. Realize how you experience this miracle every day. And now shape-shift yourself into the magnificent writer you are meant to be!

I must relate to you that this chapter came about after listening to a tape by an extraordinary humanitarian named John Perkins, called *Shamanic Navigations*. I agree with him that shape-shifting is what must occur to create a peaceful world replete with creative beings who divine health and walk away from pain. After I had listened to it, I sat in silence in my car. The tape so reminded me of the occurrence I had experienced in the Yucatán with Jaguar Woman years ago, in 1984. The circumstances that John Perkins and I each experienced were different, but they are so very similar in substance. I have found with these great shamans—in Tibet, Nepal, Australia, and North America—that many of us who are gifted with their presence and wisdom have experiences that mirror the teachings given to us, we who may never have even met except in the dreamtime.

Sorcerers never kill you. They make you kill yourself.

—LYNN ANDREWS, *SHAKKAI, WOMAN OF THE SACRED GARDEN*

# "IN THE SHAPE
# OF A PEAR"

People have said to me in the past that my writing could use more form, more plot, which I think is an interesting statement. I think that when someone critiques your work, you should always listen. However, I write from a place of experience, a place of emotion—emotion in the sense of learning about the mysteries of life, learning about the meaning of life. And when you learn something new that you haven't realized before, you have an epiphany, an incredible experience around that newfound truth or knowledge. I remember a composer who has always been one of my great favorites, Erik Satie. He was told once that his compositions, which were magical and so wonderfully melodic, slightly reminiscent of Debussy, perhaps, his compositions lacked form. So he composed a wonderful piece called "In the Shape of a Pear."

There is a woman who was my mentor, whose work was so stimulating to me and gave me tremendous confidence to write about my own frailties, my own situation in life. And I came to

realize, as she did, that we all tend to have much of the same de-
sires and inquiry in life, no matter what our race or religion, no
matter what our spirituality. We want to know the truth; we want
to know the truth about ourselves. We'd like not to be depressed;
we'd love to have great relationships; we'd like to write a great
book or whatever it is that our endeavor happens to be. And that
brings me to the subject of writing about how you feel.

To me, the greatest writing always moves into the feelings of a
person. Truman Capote's *In Cold Blood* could have been an even
greater book had he gone into more of the feelings of horror at
what had been created. Anaïs Nin spoke of this many times, and
it is part of what I feel that women in particular have to add to the
writing world. Women write about our emotions, our feelings.
Certainly, I think, if you are to look at your book as a whole, you
might ask yourself, "How have my emotions, how have the emotions of my character, been described? Are they adequately and
refreshingly new in their expression?"

You can take a character and move deeply inside that character.
You can go on a journey into that person's existence. For instance,
I have a wonderful shaman teacher who is Kuna Indian from
Panama. She is a great teacher. Her name is Twin Dreamers. Twin
Dreamers is an incredible person to explore because she has manifested within herself tremendous skill of the physical world in
terms of dreaming, in terms of supporting her existence, in terms
of being able to survive any situation, including age. Spiritually,
with the support of the other women of the Sisterhood of the
Shields, she has taught herself great abilities of the mind and of
the spirit. If she wants to describe a tree to me in a teaching, she
will become that tree.

She shape-shifts into that tree, which we have spoken about
before—shape-shifting being a process that is very applicable to-

day and not just held within the great intelligence of the shamanic world and the native peoples of the world. I think we all definitely use shape-shifting every moment of our lives; we just don't realize it. If a Zen Buddhist wants to look at a tree, he or she becomes that tree. The great haiga painters, watercolorists of Japan and China who combine painting and calligraphy with haiku poetry, become whatever it is they are painting and they have become so for centuries and centuries. It is a very old tradition. Calligraphy is related to the power and the skill of a swordsman. The secrets of the great sword hold the key to many secrets in the motion and movement of direction of the brush stroke of pen and ink. This is, in a sense, like shape-shifting. A Buddhist describing a flower coming up out of the snow would become that flower surrounded by the frozen whiteness of the snow itself, and, underneath, the moisture of the earth beginning to melt the snow, the sun beginning to shift the colors and fragrances, the coolness of winter.

And therein lies the secret of Twin Dreamers. You can go on a journey within her and discover the feelings of the mountains, the sway of a tree, the surge of the ocean, the great power of the elements and of Mother Nature. I can write a whole magnificent book about Twin Dreamers: Twin Dreamers as she sees the world, a very unusual, magical, and dreamlike perspective. Hers may be a perspective different from what you and I might see, or it may be a lot like what you or I see. Moving into her emotions, her feelings, you can begin to understand her as a shape-shifter, as a shaman woman, as a healer, as a perfected being of light.

The Zen master moves into nature as one of the greatest teachers. The Zen master understands the mind, understands the "not-doing," for instance, of writing. There is a not-doing in the process of writing. What do I mean by that—because obviously when you write you are doing something. There is a place inside yourself to which you need to get that is the still point in the middle of a storm, the silence within the chaos inside of you. It is what we call your shaman place of power. Inside that shaman place of power, a place of Buddhist or Hindu meditation, is a place of not-doing. It is a place where you allow something to come up in you and you allow the influence of other aspects of life to be revealed, things you may not have thought of because they are not of the mind. Not-doing, non-doing, is part of the body mind. Traditionally, we think with our minds, we rule with our minds, we rule ourselves and oftentimes we become victims of the mind. Eventually, we even think we are our mind, when in fact the mind is but a tool, one of the greatest tools we have perhaps but still just a tool. And when you realize this, another kind of intelligence is able to come in. We are now beginning to prove scientifically that there are many different kinds of intelligence in the universe somewhere out in the etheric field. There is intelligence in the electromagnetic field around our bodies, intelligence that is not necessarily accessible with the mind, although I believe we hold the memory of this intelligence within the mind.

The shaman place of power is known also as the *chi*. It is a place of balance, a place where, if you suspend your thinking brain-consciousness for a while and move your creative thought down into the body mind and allow it to sit there, meditate with it, this center will become quite empty and you will become still. At first, there will be much distracting brain chatter. Things will go through your head, ideas trying to catch your consciousness. This usually moves you into fear, because fear catches your attention, and that is exactly what your conscious mind is trying to do. It wants to catch your attention and get you out of the body-mind because the brain is not comfortable with the idea of anything it does not consider rational thought. But the body-mind is enormously powerful. If you can become at one with your body-mind, you will write a great, great book. And who knows where those impulses and insights come from? You cannot define them. If you define power, just like happiness, it tends to move away from you. There's no rational description for power. It just is. It is beingness. So move into that quality of being. It is quality that has a fluid movement to it.

You will find that intuition will now come in through what you feel is the sky, or the North on the Wheel. It comes through your spirit. It comes down into your power center. It also comes up from the earth, from the South on the Wheel. It has a feeling of solidity, of strength. When the two meet near the middle, in your power center, then a new kind of life is born within you. This new life is the birth of your ideas, of your thoughts, of conceptualization.

. . . [A] long wind comes, whirls into a tornado of ideas and clouds arise from the writing-brush forest. —Lu Ji, *The Art of Writing*

# TEACHING OF
# THE WINDS

Wind is extremely variable in terms of force and impact; it can be gentle and barely perceptible, and it can be devastating and destructive. Wind is a power to honor and respect, and anybody who has read my writings knows that the wind has always been my great ally.

The winds are also enormously sacred because wind is the breath of the Great Spirit. In the beginning was the word. Behind the word is the wind, the breath of God.

Language makes you very powerful. You cannot have language without wind, without breath. When we write, just as when we do ceremony, we have to be strong in our voice, as strong as the sacred beings. We do that through our choice of words and the way we use the Wind That Stands Within to express that choice of words. Symbols like sandpaintings, or *rongas,* or any kind of sacred art are really only beautiful paintings until the winds of truth enter.

There are gateways for the winds of truth to enter and gateways for them to leave. Ceremony creates a very holy sanctuary for the winds to enter, and I will urge you to make ceremony— no matter how brief—a part of your writing life. Any time you do ceremony, you must breathe into it to give it life. When the ceremony is over, you must breathe it back into yourself once again. This is an exchange of energy that makes you strong and powerful. It connects you to the Great Spirit, and you breathe the holiness, the presence of Spirit into your body.

Everybody has a wind that stands within, and this wind is a great teacher. It is a writer's wind; it writes tales to us in the air and in the sand. Acknowledging the wind that stands within is another way to have an inner connection with the divine, because spirit can enter our bodies through the wind—through sky wind, earth wind, sun wind, and moon wind. In some cultures, winds mean everything, and if somebody loses his wind he is dead. The Sisterhood of the Shields, who are my teachers in the world of spirit and shamanic endeavor, go into the desert to become the wind. They sense the color and the direction of the wind, and it heightens their awareness.

Every child who is born has a wind that stands within; it enters the body through the swirls on your fingers and toes, what we call fingerprints. If you look at your fingertips, depending on how strong your fingerprints are, you will see that there are swirls. Hold your fingertips up and you will feel them tingling. This is a strong feeling because it is where the wind enters.

The teaching of these energy swirls by which the wind enters your body offers another way of viewing the soul, of viewing your writer's soul. What makes this teaching so fascinating is its poetic and beautiful nature. For writers and other fine artists, who, generally speaking, create with our hands, the teaching of the swirls takes on an added and very important significance because this is the wind of your spirit.

One very intriguing way to experience the teaching of the swirls is to get an ink pad from a craft store and make an imprint of each of the fingers of both hands, in order, beginning with the thumb. Take these imprints to a photocopying place and have them enlarged many times, then print them out; just be careful not to make the enlargement so big that the edges and swirls get lost in the process.

Run your fingers gently over your fingerprints. What do they tell you?

The thumb is how you ascertain your own identity, who you think you are as a person. When someone holds her hand in a fist with her thumb tucked inside, that person is holding on to her identity. This may be a sign of fear or of losing one's identity, or perhaps one who doesn't want anyone to see who she is. The thumb is your identity in the world.

The forefinger is how you move out into the world. What are you going to do in life? The wind that comes in this finger is very strong. If it is not strong, this is a good thing for you to know so that you can work on making it stronger. Remember that your frailties, your places with less strength, are in reality gateways to learning, and as such they should be celebrated. Don't be afraid to say that this finger isn't strong or that you can't see the swirls. It is teaching you what you most need to learn.

The center finger is how you hold your power, how you hold energy.

The fourth finger is your spirituality and the expression of your spirituality in the world. Anything that helps you exercise your sacred intuition is a good tool.

The little finger is the family; it is very important and plays a major role in our lives.

The swirls are like pathways or trails into our soul, our essence.

They are the footprints of the wind. We touch things to know them, and innately we perceive the winds. When you touch a baby's face or someone whom you love, your touch conveys your love. I love to touch people. I remember my grandmother, who was so magnificent. She was a concert pianist, among other things, and she had great big pads on the ends of her fingers with big swirls. She was a wonderful artist and I am sure a great shaman woman. I would always touch and caress the pads of her fingertips, and I wondered whether my pads would grow if I played the piano. They never did.

But swirls have power, and knowingly or unknowingly we go to those aspects of power in ourselves or in other people. Oftentimes you will find children holding and stroking your fingers; they are looking for power. On an unconscious level, they are trying to identify your wind.

Shaman touch is about learning to use this ability to "see" with your fingers and to trust what you see and sense. Touch is so essential. Massage builds the immune system; interferon is created naturally in the body when the skin is touched.

As a writer, how do you experience the world through the tips of your fingers? Can you feel them pulsating with energy and heat when you are deeply connected to your work and the thoughts and ideas are flowing freely onto the page? The next time you find yourself communing with the muses, inspiration flowing, become aware of the heat that is moving through your fingertips. And when that heat grows cold and the words begin to slow, breathe your own breath across your fingertips and see if that doesn't revitalize some of that waning energy.

Most writers have an intuitive knowledge and understanding of all of the senses, and none is perhaps more important for the writer than the sense of touch. With every word that you write, the wind that stands within is flowing from you onto the page, and it is this connection that makes your work so powerful. The winds can work with you, joining you on your journeys. They are always there whether you ask them to come or not, so you might as well work with them! You and your writing will be so much the richer for your commitment. The wind is always trying to get your attention, so begin to acknowledge it as it crosses your path, caressing your body and lifting your hair, flowing with you into the written word.

There is a form of movement that I give my apprentices called the Shaman Dance of Power. This can be an excellent opportunity for you as a writer to work with and strengthen your connection to the winds, to the breath of the divine, to your own power and intent. When you hold your hands up to the wind, you might feel the winds coming in one finger more than another finger or another swirl. Pay attention to this and see what you can discern. It will give you an added dimension to how you view your life and your writing.

Remember that in writing, as in all sacred and healing work, you must get yourself out of the way. The conscious doubting mind is full of ego and conditioning. There is nothing wrong with ego; you need ego to make it through life. But you cannot be controlled by ego. You have to get yourself out of the way so that your writing can shine through. The great energy that is your inspiration and passion in the world comes from the divine. If you are standing in the way, if you are standing in ego, that energy can't get to you. The swirls and the wind are another way to lift yourself out of fear and out of ego and make a real connection with the divine. Take a moment each day and honor the wind.

I looked through the window of the plane. The clouds and the smudges of gray on the horizon were from fingerprints on the plastic-covered glass, not the sky. I remembered sitting on a rock-strewn mesa with Agnes Whistling Elk only a couple of days ago, in a desert wilderness, the gathering black and purple clouds warning us of a coming storm.

"I feel hollow inside," I said to her. "There's so little left inside me to hold the wind that stands within me. I pray, Agnes. I pray so hard to understand the final secrets that the clay pots and you are trying to teach me." Tears ran down my cheeks and drifted off my skin into the warm Arizona breeze.

"My little wolf," Agnes finally said, her forehead furrowed deeply, like the canyons below. "Many trails we have traveled together."

"It is like forever," I said, feeling sad and ignorant of all that I had learned and didn't know.

"It's your heart that knows what your mind has already forgotten." Agnes's face turned gentle. "Look out across this land. What do you see?"

"I see distance," I answered, sniveling.

"Do you see the future?" she asked.

"No, just emptiness." I watched Agnes's face turn younger before my eyes. A bright gleam returned to her gaze.

"How do you do that?" I exclaimed, suddenly alive with wonder.

"I believe," she said, tears of joy filling her eyes, making them even more silvery.

"You always told me not to believe in things, not to believe in all those stones I piled up, those beliefs I had." I felt dumb and confused. A gust of wind almost blew me off the rock on which I sat.

"You believed in truths outside yourself, things that you thought would heal you, ideas, gods, teachers." Agnes rested her chin on the heel of her hand. Then she held her fist over her heart. "It's in *you*, child of spirit, always radiant with life force."

"But something is missing, a chip of wisdom, a sense of wholeness, maybe a true sense of worthiness just out of reach," I cried.

"Don't you see, you will one day get out of your own way? The light is there inside you." Agnes thumped my chest and my back, behind my heart, at the same time. My place of connection shifted suddenly and the horizon changed before me. The clouds parted. How poetic, how absurd, but they really did. The setting sun obscured my vision with golden brilliance.

"Before you can heal, truly heal, you must completely and totally believe in your perfection. You must believe in your own completeness and be able, then, to share it."

"If I believe then others will believe what I already see now," I murmured faintly.

"Yes," Agnes said, pulling me to my feet. The top of a mesa is not a good place to be in a lightning storm. Two shards of lightning pierced the red earth near us. Agnes grabbed me.

"Now," she yelled, and together we rolled into a momentary ball of light descending the slope, a rendering of old and new, light and darkness, coldness and warmth melted together in a turmoil of ever-moving and continuous radiance.

The plane suddenly jolted and the fuselage groaned under the pressure of the speed of flight meeting ground in Los Angeles. My thoughts were invisible, but still and real as I gathered my luggage and jostled with other passengers and crying children on my way up the aisle.

Children, like animals, use all their senses to discover the world. Then artists come along and discover it the same way all over.

—Eudora Welty

# IN SERVICE TO
# THE MASTERS

In the season of fall, when the great bucks grow velvet on their horns, they prepare to rut, to spar with other bucks in order to win a doe, a female with which to mate. In a sense, writing can be compared to this season. As writers we grow our talent, our ability to spar with other writers, perhaps even an inflation of our egos. It's like a velvety covering over our ordinary soul, and it prepares us to mate with the creative reckoning force within us and within the universe.

Farfetched this may be, but it is really quite true. When I walk in the wilderness among the herds of deer, the ones that have grown racks of horns covered with velvet are together for a while. They rest and they communicate with one another in a beautiful way. They are separate from the females, at least as I have seen and experienced. They are separate, in a way, as writers are separate from our creativity. I think that as a writers, the bridge between the time that we realize we are writers and writing is going to be our method of expressing ourselves in the world and the time we actually pick up the tools of writing and begin to create is not unlike the time the bucks sit with their fellow stags waiting, in a sense being of service to one another. Underneath what is seen on the surface there is a testing that is beginning to grow, a kind of pushing. It shows itself to the writer as being of service in some way. And this being of service is the true bridge to your creative force.

To be of service as a writer means to take the books of your favorite authors—and I have often told people who are neophytes to take a great writer like Somerset Maugham and open the pages of *The Razor's Edge*—take the books of your favorite authors and copy them by hand, page by page until you begin to see how a master puts that extraordinary story together. Maugham wrote with his own fluid style, leading into the search for magic and the power of self within a character, his lead character, who spent his life wondering and finding the meaning of his own individual existence. Once you have copied a book like that, you know much that nobody can really teach you, not even Somerset Maugham himself because the truth of his artistic ability is not only in the words that he writes but *in between the words,* in the settings of the sentences and the paragraphs. It is in the texture and the feel of one consonant rubbing up against another and creating a sound within your spirit that changes you forever.

Vowel sounds smooth out the spirit. Consonants seem to create a tension within which an incredible heat is fanned, the heat of your story, the heat of the adventure, the fire and the soul of a work of art. So I would like you to try this. I would like you to spend a few days finding a book that speaks to you, a work of art. Then take pen and paper and write the book out page by page, copying it longhand. As you do this, don't see it as a task that you can't wait to finish. Begin to feel the author, the writer behind the words. What must someone like Somerset Maugham have been doing as he wrote his books? I use *The Razor's Edge* because it is one of my very favorites. What was Maugham thinking of? What part of himself was he expressing on those pages? What part of his soul was not yet fully developed? Where were the flaws within his writing that reflect the beauty in color within his own spirit? Remember that oftentimes beauty is created in the flaws, in the way that words are set, perhaps, and not according to the laws of grammar and normal cadence. What do you find in your author's work that shows you an indiscretion or daring to take a chance with an idea found deep inside his own heart?

One day when we were in the middle of the outback, Ginevee, my teacher in Australia, held up a crystal to the sunlight. At the time, I was in the middle of writing *Crystal Woman.* Ginevee is a teacher of the crystal dreamtime. She teaches very few, and I was incredibly proud and honored to have been among those few. She held the crystal up to the light, and it threw cascades of rainbows onto the earth, onto the beautiful red earth of Australia. She said, "See that crystals are like human beings. You hold them up to the light, and it is their flaws that create the beauty and the color, the rainbows and the meaning of their life." I asked her what she meant as I listened to the wind gathering and blowing through the spinifex grass, creating dust devils around us. She said, "Never forget that it is within the flaws of a crystal that you find the beauty, the gateways to your consciousness."

When you have a flaw, in your writing just as in your personhood, honor it, look at it and enter it as if you were crossing a bridge over a river. Move to the other side, to the source of that flaw, and heal it. In the healing of it, the rainbow becomes part of you. The light becomes part of you. Crystals have great memory. They remember those who walked before us. So I think of Ginevee's great teaching to me when I think of writing a book. And I know that the flawed characters and the difficulties that I find in choosing words that are appropriate is where I find my skill and my service. Put yourself in service to the written word. Put yourself in service to those authors who have walked before you. Listen to how they developed a concept so that it may help you find a new way to develop something perhaps similar. If you are having a hard time with the concept of service, then go into the idea of service very deeply. To know a great master, you must first be in service to the master. You get to know a master only when you have served her. You know what she needs; you know what she likes. You begin to understand, just as with crystals, how the light shines through her soul and brings love, development, and enlightenment to those around her. In service, you learn how to give yourself over to that process completely. And as you give over to that process, for instance in the hand writing of a book, word by word, paragraph by paragraph, you give yourself over completely to that author and you become good at thinking like that author.

And then you can move on to your own thoughts. How would you have written that paragraph differently? But first you have to be in service; first you have to copy the whole book and then go back over it and see where you would change things. How would you choose a word differently? Would you add a word? Would you take a word out? How would that change the meaning before you? The attitude is one of service.

The function of art is to do more than tell it like it is—it's to imagine what is possible. —BELL HOOKS

# CLAIMING THE INNER SPIRIT—A FLIGHT OF FANTASY

The slower we go physically, the faster we go spiritually. We have to slow down in order to manifest joy. Slow down to see the results of our manifestation. Take time to understand how you are creating the thought and the manifestation of your book. That understanding creates the feeling of joy. When you write, write from the place of joy.

When you feel the deepest weeping of your soul, you are experiencing the depth of a place within you where grief takes you, often a feeling of incredible emptiness or helplessness. We usually experience helplessness as one of the most important places to avoid. But helplessness is simply not true. Never. You may feel grief when you can't take care of yourself or when you can't find a way to take responsibility for your life, and that grief may feel like helplessness. And it is important to allow yourself to feel these feelings, if for no other reason than to make your writing that much richer and that much deeper.

But know that when you are writing, you are not in a state of helplessness. If you feel helpless about your writing, then you need to do something about it. When you feel helpless, you cannot feel joy. When you cannot feel joy, then where are you?

When I look at what I have written for this book, I see that it resembles a healing book for writers. Just as we can heal our bodies with deep thought, so too can we heal our writing with deep writing, where we go beyond the written word and into the landscape, the rhythm, the colors of the picture that are behind the actual paragraphs and sentences. It's a process that comes with a deep sense of commitment to what you have written, the inner feelings of the characters which you have allowed them to reclaim through the process of your story; the strength, the mystery, the courage that your characters display. It also represents a reclaiming of the writer's spirit. As you know, the characters represented in a book and the actions of the characters within a story oftentimes reflect the actions and feelings that you as the writer have, which perhaps you can't express in your own life. So writing can be a tremendous commitment to your own state of health and well-being.

Of course, you need to claim your inner spirit as being awakened and functional within your own life. Your sense of humor, your sense of play, the vision that you have as a writer oftentimes does not come through until you begin to produce your work, until your story takes an unexpected turn. Then you stop writing for a while and you think, gosh, I wonder where that came from? Where did that extraordinary expression of courage or movement or drama come from? Well, maybe you've been afraid to go into uncharted territory and what has come up is an element of risk. Can you risk through your characters an explanation of your own complexity? Dare you put into your characters that aspect of self that still may be unrecognized within your own soul?

When a writer is at this point in her writing, I find the Sacred Wheel to be an amazing form that helps her individually, completely separate from anyone else's way of expressing herself. The Wheel gives you a form with which to work, to lift off into a concept that you may not have ever explored before, aspects of yourself that you may have disowned and need to reintegrate. In certain shamanic terms, the writing of a book is a rebirth of the self in a way, and each book is a rebirth of a different aspect of that self, maybe even each chapter. Many people start out thinking that they want to write something simplistic, something purely interesting in terms of movement of plot and mystery. Simple. Simple, so that it's pure entertainment and not anything readers have to grapple with as a reflection of aspects of themselves they may be afraid to see. However, the most elementary plot can be expressed in a most readable, entertaining way—humorous, simple, very explanatory, with little of the abstract within—yet it can still have a depth to it just because the work originates in what this writer knows.

Let me explain. When I as a shaman and a healer begin to work with someone and I see what they so desperately need but are unwilling to claim emotionally, spiritually, or physically, I will hold up a mirror for the person to see himself. Whatever mirror I hold up has to do with a place within this person that accepts the possibility that healing can actually happen. When a healer does this, there has to be within the healer the absolute certainty that no matter what the problem, no matter what the dis-ease, it can be healed. It goes well beyond belief; you must know it, just as you know that if you cut yourself, your body will heal. You don't have to think about it, you don't have to worry about it, although you do have to put a little disinfectant on it! But you know that your body can heal a cut.

With that same kind of certainty, a writer has to know that the writing process will occur. If the writer has a teacher, especially a young writer, that writer must be able to see within the teacher the knowingness that perhaps the apprentice doesn't have but needs to have. The writer has to sense it within himself and within the teacher. It's a sensing that either the teacher or the writer knows a deeper aspect than maybe they are explaining. So much of writing lives between the lines. This knowing is a *knowing* that what you are writing is entertaining or fun or profound, on whatever level you're approaching the project. There needs always to be a sense of deeper thought behind every word.

In today's world, this knowing is needed because life is about growth, is it not? It's about how you ascend to a higher plane, a happier, more complete totality within your own self, within your being, within your sense of humor, within your state of abundance, within your writing. You have a knowing that what you are writing will be successful, that it will reach your readers. "I know my readers are going to have a wonderful time reading what I am saying." Even if your book is about death or mystery or romance, you can always be excited and filled with joy. Think of Federico García Lorca's poem about *duende,* or something written by Tony Hillerman in the mesas and deserts of New Mexico. These writers speak with inspiration, and the knowing that their inspiration is coming into you is a part of all this. It's a knowing that the muses will arrive and are arriving and have arrived.

You make a place within yourself for the muses to live. Usually, you work with one muse, at least I find that, although maybe you work with a crowd. I make a place within myself for that muse to live, a place of inspiration because a muse is like an antenna bringing in inspiration on the North of the wheel. Inspiration comes in from spirit, from the muses, from your relationship with nature and the subject that you have studied. All inspiration comes in through the North of the Wheel, through spirit, and is moved down through your process, through your ability, through your instrument, through the manifestation of your work of art. Putting three words together is a work of art, as far as I'm concerned, and you make a place within yourself, maybe your heart, maybe your knees, maybe your solar plexus or your mind for the muses to live.

If the muses come in a mental way in the East on the wheel, then you have a different experience than if they came in through the West, through your emotions. The muses tend to work in a rational way: when you're working out a murder plot, this person did this, and this person did that. It's very rationally oriented. You have to figure out how one step works with another. When inspiration comes in through the East, then the entire framework is filled out with the emotion on the West of the wheel. That way your writing has balance, the mind balances the emotions. Then you go up to the North of the wheel and you bring down inspiration, inspiration that gives your writing life, that animates it with the life force. You place it on paper, and in placing it on paper you manifest your dream, whatever the dream is for this work.

There is an exercise that I would like to give you for when you wake up in the morning and you are having trouble keeping going on your book or even getting started. Get up in the morning and think to yourself, as Joe Dispenza did in the recent movie *What the Bleep Do We (K)now!?,* "I am a genius and I'm going to approach this day as a genius. I am going to live this day as if I were Shakespeare," or whoever your favorite writer is. Everything that you do on this day is going to be an act through a genius mind of incredible productivity. You have the most extraordinary relationships with the written word. You have all of your emotions; your mind and your body are in tune, and you act from that place. Do not allow a thought to come in that negates this sense or feeling. Just try it. Try it for one day. See what happens. See how it feels. At the end of the day, sit down and say, "*Hmmm,* my day was different because I approached my world from a place of genius and it was different because . . ." Write down five things that were different that day from your usual life, and if this comes easily to you, try it again the next day. Plan your day as perfectly and as powerfully as you want it to be. "I am a successful, celebrated author." Maybe you have never published a book in your life, but you wake up in the morning and you say, "I am going to live my day as if I am one of the big, successful authors of my time." You pick a person and be that person.

It's interesting for me to play Einstein for a day, a genius of quantum physics and spatial understanding of the void, putting it together with an adventure into the emotional side. This is a juxtaposition of reality that is very surreal. Just live simply, or as the most celebrated romance novelist of your time or past. Whatever it is you're trying to do, find someone who is wildly successful in that endeavor and be that person for a day. How would the person act? You have millions of dollars in the bank, you have a fabulous publisher who is going to put you on the book-signing trail doing all of the big events, and you look wonderful because you're happy and successful. Sit down with your writing from this point of view and see what happens. And at the end of this day write down five things that you wrote which were different from the kind of writing you would normally do. Explore different attitudes.

When you sit down to write, adopt the attitude, "I am going to be a genius today. With words, I am one of the greatest wordsmiths alive." You sit down and you are any one of a number of great authors whom you love, maybe you are Somerset Maugham weaving an incredible story. Choose any writer of our time whom you enjoy, whom you like, writers who are still alive and whom you could enjoy imitating. See how it feels. Your book is going to be made into a movie and you're writing it with this in mind. This kind of writing will shift the plot, perhaps bring in a bit more action. Try it. Start playing little games with yourself; sit and describe your book as if you were a different writer, not yourself but another writer.

Looking at it from a different position, how would you explain your book? It might be vastly different! There is a huge difference between a Nora Roberts and an Anaïs Nin. What would be the difference in the way you would see your story if you were someone else? Look at Tom Clancy. Look at one of Dan Brown's books. You're Dan Brown. How would you approach the story? What kind of research would you do to make this story come alive? List the different aspects that you see and experience. Feel the shift inside your body. What direction do you move to on the Wheel? If you are Dan Brown and you have had a book or two or three, one of which was on the top of the *New York Times'* bestseller list for over a year, how would you approach a new subject? How would you look at things? Your books are going to be made into movies, and nothing can be more successful. Do you feel exhausted? Are you feeling relieved? Are you feeling excited?

Or are you feeling unworthy of this, that being on a bestseller list can't possibly happen to you, so why would you spend your time playing with this? Where do you feel this in your body? If you feel a resistance to playing with the concept of different sorts of success, you need to feel where it is in your body so that you can heal it. There is probably an energy knot where you feel it in your body, perhaps in your solar plexus, which is where we usually shield against something: against an idea, against a person, against a concept. So if you can meditate for a while, close your eyes, breathe deeply, bring your consciousness into your solar plexus (or wherever the energy knot is), and look around to see what kind of resistance you see. What does it look like? It might look like a fist; it might look like a dark cave. It might look like any number of symbolic things. Then become that fist or that cave and describe what you look like and what you feel like. Find out who put the fist there. Was it your mother or father, your publisher, yourself? This is a lot to ask of yourself. It's probably very unfamiliar to you, but I would suggest that you do this because if you have a resistance to success, then the better you write, the closer you are going to come to some kind of real difficulty because part of you is afraid of success and does not feel worthy.

When I work with writers, one of the essential aspects that I try to mirror back is self-worth. Self-worth is at the base of everything we do, whether we're writing or building a relationship with a loved one. If you do not feel worthy of that relationship, whether it be the characters on the pages, success in the world, abundance spiritually and physically, if you don't feel that abundance or feel that you are worthy of it, it isn't going to come to you. And if life tricks you and it comes anyway, then you're going to have a real resistance. You're going to have an energy knot that can turn into a real problem for you. So you need to identify your feelings of self-worth right away.

Try this exercise because it works well. Relax your body and mind into a state of repose. Go inside your mind, using your imagination. Wander around. Then feel the resistance and tension in your body. Take your consciousness into the areas of stress or tension and explore the energy knots, the barriers about which I have talked all through this book, because barriers are a part of the human condition of self-sabotage.

Personally, I think of the earth and our experience of life as a schoolhouse, and everything that we endeavor to do as an act of power. An act of power like your writing creates a real mirror for you and for others. We look into that mirror, and we either have the courage to see ourselves with all of our beauty and all of our faults or we're afraid to look in that mirror and never learn a thing. If you look in the mirror and you see the faults, become excited because there is something new to learn! At least you know that because of the way your father treated you, for example, you have no sense of self-worth. So get to work on it. Don't avoid it. If a problem comes up in your life, deal with it.

As Ginevee told me, "People are like crystals. People have light. You see the beautiful rainbow light that one crystal splashes across the earth. As I am holding up this crystal the sun is shining through it sending rainbows of colors. It isn't the perfection of that crystal that created those colors; it is the imperfections, the flaws within that crystal that create the beautiful exchange of light." And it's the same way with people. We have beautiful colors and differences, one person to another, one writer to another. We all express what we see differently, and some of that expression comes out of our failings, our flaws. If we were to look at those flaws and heal them, however, our beauty would be even brighter, like a diamond, because there would be no veil; there would be no barrier to that light. There would be a clarity that you may not ever have experienced before.

Let's come to that clarity; let's find it. Use your act of power as a writer as a way of becoming an even better, truer, finer writer than you've ever been. Writers say they are afraid of failing. I wonder. Perhaps they are afraid of succeeding.

To provide a healing state out of what you see as your flaws, write them down and look at them. Maybe you can even fit them onto the Wheel. Let's say that you find that your weight is a physical flaw. "I am in the worst shape, I am lazy and I don't want to work out and I will never get on that treadmill." So you have circulation or heart problems maybe. That would be on the South of the Wheel. Maybe an aspect of your flaws is that you are completely shut down emotionally. That would be on the West side of the Wheel. In the North, perhaps you are absolutely out of touch with the divine; you don't believe in it—you have a very scientific, pragmatic approach to life and you don't see the divinity or spirit in nature. There is none of that for you. There is no unmitigated light of joy from experiencing the wonder of nature, the unexplainable and the life force that animates all living things. Or in the East of the Wheel, you think life is a scientific project. Explore what you find as a spiritual development within yourself. Maybe you find you have absolutely no use for reasoning; you are lost in your emotions and you don't like to reason things out. You let somebody else do that for you. You let somebody else pay your bills and take care of the pragmatic aspects of life. You don't want to deal with them. This would be a West experience. An example of the East would be that you're completely lost in the rational mind; you live in the rational mind and are out of balance in the emotions. These are just some examples; everybody will find different aspects of self coming onto the Wheel.

Whatever you find, take a look at yourself and see where you are as a writer. See what direction you come from most of the time, or that maybe you live in one direction and write in another. Maybe there are different times when you write from different directions. That's a bit of what I do. Sitting in the center of the Wheel, I look to the North for inspiration. Then I will walk in nature. That is one of the most wonderful ways that I get in touch with what it is I'm trying to find. After I walk, I will usually go directly to the South and sit down and write some of what

I have seen from inspiration. I will write about it a little, put the manifestation of my ideas into a physical form in the South. Then I'll kind of take apart what I have written from an emotional or West standpoint, finding what I am really trying to look for here. What is the emotion of this, what is the depth of it? Is it coming from a place of love, from a place of excitement, exuberance, or depression? Where is it coming from? Then I will move to the East to balance that. I'll say, "Does any of this make any sense at all? Is there any reason for me to even write this in terms of my own way of thinking or in terms of the world and how the world thinks? Does this have any meaning at all? Does it have a reason? Have I worked out a reason?" Maybe I need to do that because what I have written is far too emotional. After I complete this process, I move back to the South and I manifest what I have just learned. Whatever opinion I come up with I begin to write, and I become that for a time.

There is a beautiful poem by William Stafford, "Why We Need Fantasy." It's from his book *A Glass Face in the Rain*:

*It's a sensational story as it slowly falls
the rain or the used up sunlight all day
onto the dim of the land where rivers have to believe.
Followed by that rain, we
hunt a cave to hide in. We try to be brave or we find,
by moving fast, the wind
that lurks in the air we breathe.
Some animals find a way to keep from being
found. They eat the days
they live that brave. Who needs a dream? That
there aren't enough caves, you know,
for animals that have our need.*

All language is a longing for home. —RUMI

## 27

# ATTACHMENT
# AND STICKINESS

There is a term in Buddhism and many disciplines called attachment. I am sure that you are familiar with the terminology. Attachment means giving yourself over to something that you own or would like to own, like things or a relationship. Oftentimes attachments can be very self-divisive and manipulative, and in turn, as in all things that approach attachment, your free will becomes a challenged issue.

In shamanism there is a powerful teaching that relates to attachment, nonattachment and writing. The first time I had ever heard this particular idea and wording was when Ruby Plenty Chiefs, my mentor, scrutinized me one day while we were canoeing up a small river in the late afternoon, a tributary off the Snake River in Wyoming. This was a long time ago, but I will never forget the moment. We were paddling together. It should have been quite wonderful, the feeling of being in unison with my extraordinary Native American teacher whose blind eyes glittered like sun shining through a fog. Using her extraordinary power, Ruby sees as well as anyone. All of a sudden, she stopped paddling and indicated for me to simply leave my paddle in the water.

"What is it?" she asked, looking at me, knowing that I was feeling a sadness that I couldn't find the bottom of.

I didn't know how to lift up the edges of my depressed feeling and heal it. I finally said, "I don't know, Ruby. I don't know why I am sad."

"You're feeling homesick," Ruby said with a quality of knowing that always startles me.

"How did you know that?" I asked. "I didn't even know myself!" But the moment she had said, "You are homesick," I took a deep breath and the sadness began to disappear. All that was left of it was a gripping sensation around my solar plexus.

Ruby reached out and placed her hand firmly over my chest and pressed gently. "There, little one," she said, "you need to sit in the very middle of your feelings of stickiness and understand what that means for you."

I explored her words in my mind and I felt the stickiness that she was describing. I was amazed at how sticky I really did feel.

"What are you stuck to?" she asked, as she paddled a few moments to keep us in the middle of the stream.

"I'm stuck to my home and my family," I said. "I miss them."

"And what a good feeling that can be!" Ruby said. "If you feel it differently."

"What do you mean?" I asked.

"If you can, feel your stickiness leave you as if you were washing honey off your fingers and you hold them up to the gentle wind, like now." She held her fingers up to the wind that was causing rivulets of light on the surface of the water.

"Feel that," she said.

I held up my hands and I felt the air between my fingers, soft and caressing like a piece of fine linen.

"There, you see," Ruby said, "that's an airy feeling. Not just because it is the wind, but because there is absolutely nothing attached to it. It is not sticky. It does not grab onto your fingers with its sweetness or bitterness. It is rustling through your fingers like wind through the leaves of a tree. And that's how you should live."

We began to paddle again and headed toward a shallow area, where we beached the canoe. We pulled the old canoe up onto the sand and sat on a rock, looking out across the stream and the high Grand Teton Mountains in the distance. The mountains seemed higher than any I had seen in a very long time, higher than the Alps in Switzerland. What a magnificent sight!

"There," she said again to me. "See. It's gone." She put her hand back on my solar plexus. "It's gone."

"Yes, it is," I said. "That tightness is gone." I realized how terrible my stickiness had made me feel, and I really had not known how to deal with it.

It was then that I truly learned to sit in the middle of my fear, to sit in the middle of anything that comes up that I don't understand with my emotions or my mind, my spirit or my physical body. I simply sit in the middle of it and try to determine how I had done such a thing to myself in the first place, because it doesn't come from outside of me, it comes from inside of me, this stickiness. It is something that I choose to do. Then I realized that writing has something to do with all of this. Writing can be enormously sticky. We become attached, sticky about what we are writing, the subject, the way we are expressing it, wondering whether we are writing it the way it should be written. Then we form an ego that creates real stickiness. We know how to do this better than anyone. Particularly if we have had some success in writing, we become sticky about the fact that we are a writer, and a published one at that.

So take a look at your ideas and your story line. Take all of that and your defensive feelings, your protective feelings, your feelings of stickiness, and go sit under a leafy, beautiful tree. Watch the leaves flutter in the wind. Feel the air through your fingers. See how nature has so much to teach you. Realize how you may be sticky about your writing or your abilities. When we become ill, we are sticky about something. Most likely if you have pain in your body, there is an aspect of your consciousness that is trying to reach you, trying to get your attention at long last so that you will listen and find your guts, your help, your strength. You can personify this consciousness that is knocking and put a face on it. You might call it an angel. I call it an ally. We all have ally energy, or an angel if you prefer, that wants to help us, a guardian of our soul. Sense whether your ally feels sticky to you. If it feels sticky, you need to explore it and free it up so that it becomes a feeling like the desert wind. Some shamans say that extreme heat or extreme cold bring you to a state of enlightenment. That is something to meditate on.

As a writer, as an artist, as a person who is living in this world, what are you really trying to accomplish? What is that dream that you have? Are you living it? What ideas have you become sticky about? Politics often lead us to a distraction of stickiness. We become so desperately fired up over one situation or another. If we have a teacher, our teacher is better than any other teacher. If we have an agent or publisher or idea, it is always better than anyone else's. Those are sticky things. Illness is a sticky thing. Fear, the barriers to writing—clarity, fear, power, aging—all are things about which we can get very sticky, become sick over, even die over because we don't know how to look at them properly.

That day that I was with Ruby we talked together for a long time about my life. She asked me many questions about my feelings in terms of home and family. I discovered that my insecurity and loneliness as a child made me always look for the answers and repercussions of that loneliness and the isolation. When I was young, we moved constantly. Perhaps that is another reason that stability and home mean so very much to me. We talked about that. I realized that I was very sticky about territory, the territory that I considered my world—my friends, my people. Of course, they are not "my people." We are people who share a given space.

As a writer, I try to observe and experience the world with as much passion as I know how to find and bring the glitter and light of that experience into my words. I try to choose words that don't jump out at you, that are not difficult to understand. Perhaps that is a mistake, because I think it is a tragedy that we don't use the English language as well as we possibly could. I want to speak very well, but I also think that trudging through huge, obscure vocabulary is a disappointment to a reader and takes the reader away from the flow of what it is that you are really trying to say. Of course, this is a generality, so there is a great untruth in it, because sometimes only certain words will do, particularly words like *pejorative* that sound so much like the negative quality that they express. Words are magnificent. Etymology is fascinating to me. It is the way that you use those words that is so important. If you are trying to impress people with your knowledge and wisdom, then perhaps you should look again at your stickiness. Stickiness is illness, sadness, low energy, fatigue, not being able to sleep, not being healthy, not being motivated; it is jealousy, feeling ownership where it is inappropriate. All of these are stickiness.

If you were a dog, what kind of dog would you be? Or would you rather be a cat or an eagle? Or a horse? If you were to choose what we call a power animal, an animal that represents your instinctual nature that you don't express, what would that animal be? What would you discover about yourself? Dream on that as you move into sleep and become unsticky. Dream that you are an eagle or a raven, or a little mouse that knows the secrets of the earth. Dream that animal as you. Where does it take you? What does it want to teach you? Incidentally, we can be very sticky about writer's block, when we go, "Oh, I'm stuck and can't go any further." Remember that we talked about taking a different fork in the road. Maybe that is a good time to talk with your power animal and see what you can discover.

Truth is what works.   —WILLIAM JAMES

# RISK-TAKING AND
# LAZINESS OF THE SOUL

Through my own experiences, I know that the antidote for
laziness, whether it be spiritual or physical, is risk. What do
I mean by risk? Risk is something that people may see very differently. Some people say that they take a great risk by joining a
school because school costs money, and in order to afford it, they
have to be very careful. That is one kind of risk.

The kind of risk about which I am speaking is not parachuting
or mountain climbing, physically dangerous sports. And it is not
necessarily financially challenging, although it often is. Risk happens, as it has in my life, when you find that your work, your growing consciousness, what you are doing in the world of spirituality
(whether shamanic or otherwise), takes you far away from where
you are now, from the people you have always known. You may
even find that your mate seems like a stranger. And you choose to
make a decision, perhaps about your mate or your job, or about
certain friends. You realize deeply that people who try to hold

you back and are not happy about your growth are not truly your friends. When this happens, you are at a place of decision, a cross-roads where you have to choose to leave or else to love them un-conditionally. But whatever your choice, you put them in a corner of your life.

The kind of risk I am speaking of has to do with living on the edge of your awareness, where you truly push the envelope of all possibilities that come to you. Leaving a mate, for instance, is a tremendously dangerous situation, particularly for women. If a woman hasn't worked and has children, she doesn't necessarily know how she is going to survive. Oftentimes she makes the wrong decision because of survival concerns. Maybe that is wrong, maybe it isn't. Maybe it's a teaching. It depends on the situation completely.

Laziness is a very interesting subject. Laziness isn't necessarily apparent on the outside to people around you. Laziness can be something that is of the soul: it is much easier not to believe in life transformations or in enlightenment. When you believe that enlightenment is not real and you put the experience of enlight-enment into a little corner of your life, and yet you continue to pray and bring spirit into your life, you are trying to create a sit-uation in which you don't really have to take responsibility for what you believe, you don't have to take responsibility for shifting and the change that is inherent in living a sacred life. I think a lot of people want to believe that they can lie on the floor on a nice soft pillow and meditate to create order in their lives. Not so for the writer! This is simply not so. How are you going to get any-thing written lying on a nice soft pillow on the floor? And I have news for everyone: the shift is not going to happen if that is all you are doing. People ask me over and over again, "Why can't I go out in my dream body?" The reason they cannot is because they have not done the work. Their intent is lazy and most likely not strong.

Not long ago I gathered my teachers around me and we talked at great length about how we sabotage ourselves with laziness. What we decreed was that the antidote for laziness truly is risk!

How do you risk in your life? How do you push the boundaries of your existence past what you ever dreamed you could be or do in your life? It's like being a skier heading down a slope you have never been down before, hoping that you have the ability to make it to the bottom in one piece. That is what this challenge is like, if you really do apply yourself, if you really are into evolving your consciousness. You proceed from a place of passion and a desire to become enlightened in this lifetime and, you hope, in the next couple of lifetimes.

The real issue here is to understand the source of power. Power does not come from wandering between this belief and that in a dilettantish way. Power comes from an extraordinary experience that you may have and share. The power is in it because you have lived it, and that is what I want you to see. This isn't a belief structure. It is a process of understanding where power lives. You have to do the work, and you have to have the experience for power to come to you. I'm saying this out of a place of absolute love for this study, for my magnificent teachers who are very much alive and kicking in this world, and for my care for you. Remember this concept of risk, wiping away the laziness of spirit. Human beings are by nature lazy. This is not a judgment of you. I'm as lazy as the next person, and I had to learn to take my power. I had to learn to risk. I had to learn to understand the importance of overcoming not only the laziness of the physical but also the laziness of spirit.

We all experience power differently, but experience power you will do if you exercise your intent. Experience power you must if you are to become a successful writer. There is a reason why I have papers and activities for the apprentices in my Mystery School to do. There is a reason I have suggested exercises for you to do throughout this book. That reason is to help you exercise your intent and your will so that you can move into those domains of power and elegance where you so much want to live. I do believe that this whole subject is part of the way that we block ourselves from the deepest experience that we could possibly have. If you question your instincts or the very teacher that you have, even though you know somewhere deep in your heart and in your soul that this is the place you need to be, then what is underneath your striving and your working and your dedication is a terror of becoming what you are trying to become. There is a terror of taking your power.

Doubting is another way, causing negativity and conflict. Doubting is really a defense against going deeper into your own power, recognizing your power, taking your power. It is a defense against your own realization. This is not to say that all of the work you do with nature spirits and your guardians, with all of the fantastic concepts and ideas and creativity that come through your ceremonies, is not powerful. It is not to say that all of the writings you have done are not wonderful and powerful, because many of them are. But it is the act of creating what you receive through your inspirations that is important. That is where you come face-to-face with your will to risk and overcome laziness. And you as a writer know the difference, because as a writer you are probably also a reader and you know the difference between a writer who comes just from ideas and a writer who has made the journey into inspiration and deep communing with the muses, with her allies and her spirit and her intent in order to bring back her work.

You can't just dream. You have to manifest the dream.

Most people invite the guests and furnish themselves as the meal.

— LYNN ANDREWS, *JAGUAR WOMAN*

# 29

# DEALING WITH
# CRITICISM

At some point in your life, you are going to meet someone who doesn't like you simply because you are blond or brunette, or you're a man and not a woman or you're of a different race or religion, or maybe just because they don't like the way you look. It is the same way with writing. You write something with everything that you are, from your heart and from your soul. You try your best and send it out there. But some people don't like it. And you feel from the depths of your being that they don't like you, because so much of you is in your writing. When I began writing, I wrote about an unusual subject with unusual wording. It was about the most intimate frailties of my life. People spoke about my autobiographies as if they were speaking about somebody else. When I would say, "But *she* is *me*," there was no point of understanding.

I think when you are criticized as a writer, it is one of the most painful journeys because so much of you goes into your writing.

One thing that my teacher Agnes Whistling Elk said to me early on, as I was moaning and groaning about some book review, was, "You know, Lynn, you must be doing something right or they wouldn't be talking about you." I argued with her, saying that couldn't possibly be. Later, only later, did I realize the truth of her words.

If you write something that changes people in some way and brings them to a new place within themselves, they shift and see life with a little different light than they ever have before. Some shadows are brought forth. Oftentimes the implication of that shift is that they don't like the mirror it creates. They don't want to look in the mirror you presented, where you have had the courage to change, where you have had the courage to write, where you have had the courage to put yourself on the line and maybe they haven't. So often criticism, maybe unbeknownst to the critic, comes from a place of insecurity within the critic. Critics get so angry sometimes. Then you as a writer sit in wonderment at the array of controversy your writing has caused, depending on what you are writing and how much of your own truth you have had the courage to speak. So often your truth goes against the grain of somebody else. This disagreement is actually a beautiful thing. It is what makes the world go 'round. Yet so many people don't see it that way. They hate one who doesn't agree with them, and they won't hear of another subject or another idea or concept.

As a writer, you will be faced with this criticism at some time. Either your work will be criticized or you will be criticized. That is a time to be humble. Instead of getting your hackles up or sitting in complete disbelief at the strange things that come from people, it is essential that you go into that place of humble knowing within yourself and understand deeply that we all come from different backgrounds, from different dreams, perhaps from different areas of learning in this lifetime. We cannot all agree or be the same. Life would be very boring. This is when you ask yourself to be a warrior, someone who understands her own circle of power and does not allow anyone else to step into that circle of power. In writing, you have gone beyond that circle. You have put something out there and people can do with it as they will. It is necessary that you understand your own circle of power and stand within it. This is all you need for your own happiness, for your own accomplishment, for your own bliss. If you can appreciate this at a deep level, you will realize that oftentimes compassion can be a part of self-importance.

When you spend a lot of energy holding up an ideal, propping it up in the world so that people see this person you think you are—which is, of course, a very illusory concept to begin with—you lose a great deal of energy in the process. You want to be accepted. You want to be seen as the extraordinary person you think you are. In this process, you lose most of the energy that you need for the dreaming from which writing comes. You need dreaming. It is a part and a result of your energy body. Your energy body is not your physical body. It is around your physical body. That energy body is what enters into the play of life, enters into your creativity, enters into your growth as a human being. Without that energy body, you will have a pitiful life, a small and pitiful existence.

When you are criticized, take a look at who it is you are trying to be. Who are you propping up out there in the world, who maybe doesn't exist at all except in your own mind? Or maybe you are real, creative, a magnificent person. Whoever you are as a writer, own it and be proud of your perceptions and your willingness to write and to grow. My intent in writing this book is to help you do just this.

I don't feel sympathetic toward some characters, unsympathetic toward others. I don't love some characters, feel contempt for others. They have attitudes. I don't. —Don DeLillo

# DEATH, DREAM BODY, AND BARRIERS

## DEATH

There is a famous line from a poem by seventeenth-century English poet John Donne: "Any man's death diminishes me, because I am involved in mankind, and therefore, never send to know for whom the bell tolls. It tolls for thee."

In other words, when you surrender to your writing, it is as if you are surrendering to a master or maybe even to a love. Lovers die into each other, as I have written about in *Shakkai*. Only those who are ready to face death can love because love is a kind of death. And death always implies love.

Death comes in many ways beyond your actual death. It comes in what some people call "little deaths"—the deaths of being frightened, of being in an accident, falling in love, and even of writing a book. To my way of thinking, that is the reason why so many people find writing an agonizing process, which all of us have gone through. No matter how much we love to write, some aspects are agonizing because of the mirrors writing creates. What this means is that if you are going to write something powerful, there is an aspect within which you die to that work. You become completely reborn. You become something very new, not the same person walking away from your writing desk as the person who arrived there. This is very scary for some people. Many writers would rather never face it. That is their choice. But if you are going to make that choice, then know on a conscious level that you are making it. For example, some people make a choice not to have any sexuality in their lives. That is perfectly fine, but it is a choice that they must know they are making. It is the same with making the choice not to die to your writing, because your work is going to have very different results depending on which way you choose. And so it is a choice you must make on a conscious level.

If you are going to write a book, you face many little deaths. You die into your project. You remove yourself in many ways from the life that you ordinarily live. It is a joy, because you find a place of stillness and bliss within you. There is a whole other part of yourself that becomes born right before your eyes, and you can animate that new being or choose not to. It is frightening if you choose to do so, because you may fail. You may not be up to the task, and that's okay, too. If I were in this position, I would look at it as a challenge from Great Spirit and I would move into it with everything that I am. And that is dangerous.

## DREAM BODY

There is a part of ourselves that I talk about in my trainings in shamanism called the dream body. The dream body, that dreaming part of you, can be dangerous. It loves danger because then it becomes tested. You begin to learn what you are made of, and it is a mirror that many are afraid to look into. In ancient Mayan teachings there is something called a smoking mirror. When you look into a smoking mirror, you look into an aspect of self that fights with self, that fights with you, that wants to win over you, even though it is an aspect of your own being. Within that fight there is heat and energy and disruption and terror and a new beginning. When you fight with that smoking mirror, look at who it is that is fighting against your writing. Someone within you is fighting against that writing. Something in you wants you to fail. There is something in you that is the very opposite of the aspect that you are trying to develop. In other words, if you feel insecure in your writing, then perhaps there is an ally in your writing that is the part of you that wants you to be powerful. Your ally is trying to help you to be successful by testing you, to make you strong.

The ally in you helps you build a dream body. It helps you see yourself and helps you manifest your truth. This is a warrior teaching. It is a teaching of how to approach life as an ecstatic, joyous being.

## BARRIERS

To become that joyous being, to become that great writer, you have to face many barriers. My old friend Carlos Castaneda wrote about barriers to perception, and it was one of the things on which we agreed. Don Juan Matus, a Yaqui shaman in the Sonoran desert of Mexico who was Carlos's teacher, talked about four barriers. One of the barriers he described is the barrier of clarity, clarity being your perception in a balanced way. The next barrier is the barrier of fear. The third is the barrier of power. The fourth is the barrier of aging. For many years I have felt these barriers come up in my writing life, and I think it is important that we explore them within ourselves as writers.

To me, the barrier of clarity is a block in your perception of what you are trying to write, and it can come up often in your spiritual work as well as in your writing. When you are up against the barrier of clarity, you begin to become unbalanced; you don't know what your spiritual work or your writing work is, or how to balance it with your everyday work. How do you balance the dream world, your writing, and your inspiration with making money?

When you are unbalanced, it is very difficult to write your characters or resolve situations in a way that is credible and meaningful. When we are writing, we become obsessed and possessed by the writing, and as a result, we begin to ignore our physical bodies. We sit for hours and don't move. We need to remember that muscles hold memory, that the muscles of our bodies are a source of a great deal of inspiration. We think inspiration comes only from the ethers, but often it comes from the memories that are held in our bodies, as Dr. Ida Rolf showed so beautifully in her massage treatments. She would go deep into someone's tissues and help release memories that were causing energy knots and pain. Being "Rolfed" would be a wonderful thing for the writer! Deep tissue massage can be very painful, but there are many techniques of massage, including Dr. Rolf's, that help us to move into heightened states of perception, especially when we are writing. For instance, you can begin to see different perspectives around your characters, different motives or strategies that perhaps you have lived in your own life. And everything becomes clearer. Everything becomes more balanced between your creative mind and the actual physical writing and development of conflicts within your characters.

When you come up against the barrier of clarity, what you are trying to write about becomes unclear. Look at this as a challenge. It is a good thing, not a bad thing. It is a challenge to see what it is in yourself that is scrambling the way you think, that is making it impossible for you to hear the radio waves, those points of inspiration that normally come very clearly. Sit in the middle of it and look at it. What you will see is much like watching a pond become clear of mud and leaves after something stirs it up. Clarity comes. But patience is needed.

When Don Juan spoke of the barrier of fear, he spoke of the warrior, the hunter, the stalker, and the dreamer, which are all aspects of your power. As my teachers have said to me in so many different ways, when I have fear, I have a way of sabotaging my happiness and my success as a woman of power.

You may write ten magnificent chapters, and then nothing else comes. This is when you find the forked trails, the crossroads of power. As the warrior, the hunter, the stalker, or the dreamer, you the writer have to make a choice to go down a different path, one that is unfamiliar, or you give in to the barrier of fear. This is one of the reasons that writers sometimes are frightened of death, because there is a death process in creativity. You as a writer have to choose a path that is different perhaps from any you have ever been on before, and that is scary. But you must make the step into that new path for your writing to be complete.

To me, fear can be an addiction. When we have fear, we sabotage ourselves. Fear undermines us. For the writer, there are two important fears: recognition and financial support. Not many people are lining up to patronize or support the writers in the world. Good writers are often left out of the literati, left out of the clan, and ostracized from the lists of successful writers. Once in a while, though, someone gets through!

Fear of not being able to support one's family is probably a very realistic concern. Not so many people become wealthy as writers. But you don't write for money. You don't do what you *do* for money. Donald Trump explained this very well: "I don't make deals for money. I make deals because I so enjoy the process. I love making deals. It's how I get my kicks in life."

Writers write because we wish to produce. Your writing is what you do. It is how you say the many things that are important to you. You do this through your characters and through your writing genre, fiction or nonfiction. If you start focusing on the finished product—the amount of money you will make or whether you will be accepted or famous—you are lost. This is just not what writing is about. The outcome is an addiction, too. For me, it is an ally sitting on my shoulder, saying, "So you want to write? I'm going to test you and see how you handle this."

Most writers have been plagued by these thoughts. When they come, you need to take hold of your ally and say, "This isn't me. This isn't what I'm going to do, it's not what I was meant to do with my writing." I write because I love what I do. It is not an obsession or an agony, although there may be moments of agony when I wonder, "Is this good? Can I really write about this? What will happen when I do?" Remember that the allies do test what we are made of. Are you made of something real, or are you just a bag of wind?

Fears of all kinds present themselves to the writer. Sit in the middle of your fears and face them. In fact, give them a face. Look at the aspect of the smoking mirror that is trying to fight against your success. Name it. Look at it. What does it have to teach you? Learn what that is and you'll be able to go on. Don't let the allies trick you into losing sight of your target, which is writing. When you come up against the barrier of fear, that is when you need to take hold of your ally and say, "This fear isn't me and I'm not going to allow it. This fear has nothing to do with what I was meant to do; it's only a barrier which I can overcome."

The next barrier to your writing power is power itself. Power is a deadly barrier because as human beings we tend to fall in love with ourselves very easily. How many times have you read the work of a writer and you know that writer is in love with his own words? That writer is not in love with the process but rather with her own majesty. You do not want to become known as a writer who is in love with your own majesty and not with the writing process. Remember that in true majesty there is grace and within that grace is the gift of humbleness. With it, you don't feel a sense of separation from the world because of the power and the magnificence of your writing. Rather, you feel a oneness. Feeling a oneness with your power is a beautiful thing.

Understanding that you do have power requires taking responsibility for it. This is the essence of true power. You sit in the middle of your power, in the middle of your writing with grace, with humbleness, and with responsibility for who you are and what you have written. Then you radiate out from your center with love, as a writer of power. When you move into any other description of power, which we do because we have frailties, remember once again that it is your ally testing you. You need to pass this test each and every time you come up against it.

Let's say you have an ego about what you write. Somebody comes up to you and says, "You know, I hear your words and they are magnificent, but why don't you try to do this and such?" Then you feel a barrier coming up inside you. You don't want anybody to tell you what to do. You don't like it, because you know what you want to do. If something comes up inside you that feels like this barrier, it is most likely power testing you in the form of ego. And your ego is the mind trying to hold you back. Try to look at that when you have an ego about your writing. When an editor comes in and red lines eight paragraphs that you think are the best you have ever written, take a look at it and make sure that you are coming from a place of true creativity and not ego.

Oftentimes in my work, when I speak about moving into awareness and higher consciousness, I talk about power as an entity of energy that tests us, because truly that is a reality. That is exactly what happens. Power tests you to see if you are worthy of it, to see if you are worthy of moving on. Abe Lincoln once said, "If you want to see what someone is made of, give him power."

Let's say someone you know has produced a magnificent body of work and has reached the pinnacle of success that is power—power in money, power in recognition, power in every way in life. Strangely enough, this is when fear may well enter, for that is when power takes a really good look at a person. If that person is you, you may find that you develop a good case of what people call writer's block, which becomes a kind of terror because you lack true self-esteem. To me, that is losing touch with clarity and with balance. Your lack of a sense of self-worth drives you into the great barrier that is born of the emotions, of not living in the now, the barrier of ego, of ego mind and low self-worth. In my opinion, the most powerful dictators that have ever lived, the Hitlers and Stalins of the world who murdered millions of people in the name of "ideals" that they considered to be right, really murdered those who came up against them because of their deep and abiding lack of self-esteem. They stood at the crossroads of power and could not pass the test; they succumbed to fear.

Many people have a moment of fame and become obsessed by

that fame. It becomes an addiction. It is like being possessed by the martini that one is drinking, possessed by the spirit of the martini. You don't possess the martini; it possesses you. It is the same with power. Do you possess power or does power possess you? All people who have creative ability and power face this in the mirror every day. Look at it as your ally, your power testing you. Are you made of the stuff of genius, or are you ego-driven and just afraid of losing power?

A writer, any person with true power, is never afraid of losing that power. You simply sit in the middle of it. You are made of it and you radiate out from it, just as if you are made of light. When you are made of light, you are never afraid of losing light because you are light. Can you imagine the sun saying, "I'm so afraid of losing my brilliance?" You are not going to lose your brilliance, for you *are* that brilliance. Once you sit in the middle of your writing with grace, with humbleness, and with responsibility for who you are as a writer and what you have written, then you are a writer with true power. This is a test that you must pass every time you come up against it.

The last and most difficult barrier that you will use to sabotage yourself is aging. This is the last barrier that Carlos and Don Juan talk about. And certainly aging is irrefutable, because we all age. But we have somehow made this strange agreement that we are going to *get* old. Even though we rebuild the cellular body every seven years, we seem to agree that our DNA isn't going to repro- duce as it did in the very beginning, that suddenly we will have wrinkles and gray hair and we will shuffle around.

Is that a fact? Let me share my experience with my teachers. These forty-three women have evolved past the aging process. They don't accept that agreement. They have shifted out of a dream body that accepts aging as truth. Theirs is a cellular DNA shift and a true change. They have learned to be true consummate dreamers, so they go beyond the physical world of relativity and what the relative world really means in the process of time. They go beyond the veil every day. They know how we really exist. It doesn't matter if you believe me or not about these women. The fact is, however, that I have experienced this as a result of our relationship together. I can share it with you. Even though it sounds completely irrational, perhaps it will tickle your curiosity enough to think about it. And then think about what you are really doing to your life through your agreement on aging.

One wonderful thing about writing is that we can always write. But we become afraid that maybe we have lost our chops. Maybe we aren't as good as we used to be, maybe younger people want something different. People say, "Well, I am seventy years old and I am still not recognized. I have arthritis and can't hold a pencil. I don't own a computer." There are realities in life that present huge challenges, yes. But there is an Old Wise One inside you. Contact that Old Wise One in a meditation with yourself in a beautiful place in nature. Take your writing with you and talk to that Old Wise One. Ask the Old Wise One how you can heal this fear that you have, this aging, this lack of energy. You are bleeding away your energy by thinking of aging in the first place. I want to tell you, my dear writer friend, that aging in this time in human life is a privilege, not a curse.

Aging is an extraordinary ally. As you age, you have developed your self-esteem. You have walked through many gateways of initiation in your writing. As you grow older, you become more aware of the balance in nature, and your energies are not wasted on youthful dilemmas. Your beauty becomes a beauty of a different kind. You contain a wealth of knowledge and you become a wise elder writer. This all depends on your attitude.

## MIRRORS

We are dreamers and we can shift the dream body in the process of dreaming. We dream every night, but oftentimes we don't remember our dreams. We can learn to let go of our beliefs and the conditioning that says we can't dream and go out of body. This is something that may be difficult to believe until you have experienced it. But it is something that you most definitely can experience if you will allow yourself to be open to the possibility.

You may surmise the dream body or feel it deep in your soul, and somehow you know that it is true. So you follow a thread. You follow a story. Somewhere deep inside you know that my experiences of dreaming are true. When I first read Carlos Castaneda, I knew his story was the truth. Many people could not believe it, saying he couldn't prove it. I knew that the thread of truth was there, that he had gotten hold of a story or a story had gotten hold of him, and he had to take it to the end. And he did. The same thing happened with me.

I asked for teachers. My teachers and my teachings are very different from Castaneda's. But there are certain truths that are intertwined in all teachings. Castaneda speaks of the barriers to perception, dreaming, and every aspect of our life. These are the same for everybody no matter what your belief system may be. When you move into that extraordinary world, there are barriers to be met, because you want those barriers to test you and to make you stronger. You want to be a better writer. You want to take on what is powerful in your life. You are not a shy little person sitting in a corner afraid to face the world. I was one of those people. I have told you, it was very difficult for me to do beginning, middle, and end of anything. I was so frightened when I faced the writing of *Medicine Woman*. I went through what we call shaman death, which is ego death. And that was just the beginning of a very treacherous journey. But I had asked for it in some way, so I took it on. I had courage. I was determined to divine the teachings and share them, and that is what I have done. That is the kind of commitment you need for your work.

A woman once came to me, crying, "I only want to write a book on gardening." I told her that gardening was one of the most sacred things we can do. The sacred lotus blossom grows out of the murky depths into the magnificent perfection of a flower and the symbol of enlightenment. Gardeners sow seeds, and from those seed beautiful flowers grow. As writers, we sow seeds, and those seeds sprout our writing, sprout our soul. All of these seeds are sown within the soil of our accomplishments, our failures, our frailties, the heartfelt indignities, and the beauty that we have all experienced. A book on gardening—teach me how to plant, teach me how to grow, teach me how to nourish a garden—is a book about the garden of the soul.

As a beginning writer, you can feel endlessly that the great works of art in writing have already been done. Why should I write a book on women's feelings and emotions? Anaïs Nin has already done it. Vanessa Redgrave told me years ago that she never went to see movies while she was making a movie because she would compare herself and feel less than what she really was. And I thought, "My gosh. She is one of the great actresses of her time. Why would she not want to see movies?" Then it occurred to me that no matter how great we are, we are all—writer, architect, actor, artist—still human and the mirrors that we create in the process of creating something new are forever leading us toward our enlightenment. Never compare yourself with another writer because in a sense we all are overshadowed by someone like

Shakespeare. However, it is also true that you are an individual. Your experience is different from that of anyone else who has ever lived, and your work is powerful and unique because of who you are. You would not be writing in the first place if you did not have the writer's spirit, and that is a treasure beyond compare, which gives you vision and awareness deep inside your soul that no one except yourself can ever take away.

I think that it is very important as writers to sit and work with our barriers. I have certainly spent most of my apprenticeship facing these incredible structures that I had built to inhibit myself. We all do. Your writing is a mirror. A mirror is something that you create in the world that reflects you back to you, no matter what the subject is. Many of us are afraid to look in that mirror, because so often what we write is so much more than what we are or think we are. As I have said so many times, you sometimes have to grow to that writing and scramble like mad to keep up with it, to take the power that is given you and not be seduced by it. You are challenged to define your clarity and perceptions every day to see if they are true. You are challenged to work with your fears. You look in the mirror and see this ugly, distorted creature that is you, faced with terror at just the thought of publishing your book. The mirror may reflect a dilettante who can't do beginning, middle, and end, asking, "How do I finish this book? How do I stop writing just one sentence at a time and start writing an actual book?" Or it may reflect the face of a poet. Poets speak differently from novelists because poets see things on such a vast scale, and they distill it into the essence of what the meaning truly is. Poets often write one sentence at a time.

My agent, Al, has always told me, "Lynn, whether you are older or younger, you can always write. It doesn't matter." And he is right. So you become an old writer! One good thing that happens over the years is that you never outgrow writing. Just because you are ninety doesn't mean you outgrow writing. It's all in how you look at aging. All aging means is that you have probably lived a long time. You see your physical body begin to shift, moving closer to Mother Earth. You work three times as hard as you did in your twenties to keep in good physical shape. You begin to get tired. So many elder people have said to me, "I am so tired, I don't want to go on. I don't want to keep doing this. Why am I doing this? I just want to retire." Usually a writer won't say this. It is more likely to come from a teacher, an insurance person, somebody in a field that they don't think is creative. They don't realize that every field is creative.

I work a lot with people, helping them to take their consciousness inside themselves and find out where all of these points of view come from. Remember that we are just a point of view acting upon the world. What is your point of view? Are you trying to make the world a better place, or are you living within the soul of negativity and within the sorcery of the spirit of aging? The spirit of aging needs to be confronted by the Old Wise One within you, and the Old Wise One is magnificent. All of my teachers, for the most part, are very elder, and they shape-shift from one element to another, from one figure to another. They are consummate shamans. If you go to the Himalayas, you find the circle around the Dalai Lama shape-shifting.

One of my beautiful shaman teachers, Twin Dreamers from Panama, now lives in the north of Canada most of the time, and she shape-shifts almost every time I see her. She is the one who told me that stories stalk you. I always thought stories came from me. We always think we own our ideas, when, in actuality, we share our ideas. I share my ideas with others, and they share their ideas with me. We give thoughts and ideas away because they are part of the oneness of consciousness. We don't even own our life force because it's part of the oneness of existence. My beautiful teachers in the Sisterhood of the Shields would never conceive of saying that they own their teachings. They know that these teachings are to be shared, and how people use them is really up to them. We all use them in different ways. Castaneda, for example, saw barriers as barriers to perception. I see them as barriers to shamanhood, to writing, because I think that writing is a sacred art and a great force. Once you decide to become a part of that great force, then a kind of testing occurs and the ally is really needed. And that is why I have written about allies. You need your ally so that you know when you are being tested and when it is just yourself getting in your own way. We tend to sabotage ourselves, particularly if we were abused kids. Marie-Louise von Franz wrote of this in *Puer Aeternus,* which is Latin for the "eternal child." If you were an abused child, not necessarily physically abused, you tend to sabotage your success as you grow older. You can learn to look at this in terms of power, not power over someone but power as an aspect of the integrity of your character and your ability to manifest your dreams.

For every moment of light there is a moment of darkness and one defines the other. Therefore, if you have tremendous light in the world, you will attract darkness, like moths are attracted to a flame. But that does not mean that you should be frightened or that you should shield yourself. It is simply a process of standing in your own power and knowing your own boundaries, which is taking your power. Taking your power is an aspect of defining your boundaries. Somebody crosses those boundaries, and you have the right to do whatever is necessary to get them out of there. Your allies, however, stand with you and they question. They ask if you are worthy. And you need to question them because finally you have to take your power.

People think that creativity is like stories, that it is outside of them.
But it inhabits you like your own life force and it animates your being.
Creativity is within the crystal palace of your mind.

—LYNN ANDREWS, *THE POWER DECK*

## 31

# ALCHEMY

D o we really think that as creators we own our ideas? I was
thinking of a wonderful book called *The Coming Race,* by
Edward Bulwer-Lytton. It's an old book, written at the turn of the
last century. It speaks of the world inside the world inside the earth.
It speaks of a race of people, humans who have lived within the
heartbeat of Mother Earth, different from we who live on top of the
earth feeling the heartbeat of Mother Earth under our feet. What
kind of change would that produce within us, I wonder. What kind
of shift?

That would be like standing at the crack between the worlds.
We stand on the earth feeling the power of the earth churning
beneath us. If we have a sense of power, we feel the stillness and
the emptiness, and yet, not unlike a washing machine, it doesn't
seem to be moving. But if you place your arms around the machine, you can feel the turbulence within.

There is also a world of higher consciousness, of other dimen-

sions or parallel realities, of superconsciousness or superego or su-
premacy of the higher mind, depending on whom you are speaking
with. What it means is that there is more to life than what we see.
I think that this has been proven by quantum physicists and by
masters throughout the world. It has been proven by ourselves
and our need always to place God outside ourselves, always placing the supreme being not within us but underneath us, above us,
around us. But surely not within us!

Why is it that we seem to place such a reverence for everything
but ourselves as creators? On the front of *Time* magazine not long
ago there was a picture of a sacred person looking for spirituality,
the essence of power, outside the self. Is it in the blood? Is it in
our cellular structure, in our DNA? For so many millennia we have
placed God outside of ourselves. The extraordinary cosmology of
our being could not be part of the ordinary world; it has to be
outside of the ordinary world. So how, then, do we travel from
the ordinary world to the other world, if that is the agreement? In
my world of writing, of creativity, of healing and helping others
heal themselves, how do I approach that?

I approach that with an ally. The ally is the bridge, as I have mentioned before, between the ordinary world and the creative force in
the universe, the creative self who is accessible to you as a creative
person, as a writer, an artist, a person who creates something out
of nothing. When you use your ally, whether it comes in the form
of Jesus, the guardian angel, or the black grizzly bear, elk or eagle,
in whatever voice it comes to you, the ally helps you not only to
ground in the ordinary world but also to know things that other
people will never know: the world on the other side; the parallel
reality. Some of us come to this incredible epiphany or inspiration
through food, through—as many sorcerers call it—the devil weed,
the big smoke and the little smoke of alcohol or drugs of some

kind. Some people find this extraordinary other world through nature; through speaking in front of a large crowd; through dance, ballet, music. We go into that other world transformed, suddenly able to open a third eye and have visions that we can't have, it seems, in ordinary life with the stress and all that encompasses.

So I would like you, as a writer, to look at your ally, the ally that in fact comes to you and moves you from one paragraph to another, from one word to another, lifting those words into melody, into harmony that you can hear, that you can feel and see and taste. Your words become enlightened words, words that may or may not follow a synchronicity of reason. But words that lift you beyond the ordinary nonetheless, beyond the mundane into something special. No matter who reads these words, they will feel a shift, a change inside themselves, which is what we've been talking about rather endlessly here. But it can never be said too often.

To me, in my world of embracing the mystery, deeply immersed in the magical and the world of power through extraordinary events, I ask you to explore the ally. Think of when you find your inspiration. Where are you? What are you doing? Are you in a restaurant, detached from the crowd? It is certainly in the moment, but where do those moments take you? What kind of movement do they imply? What kind of body feelings do you have in that moment? Your body can take you there, you know. The body is gifted with a knowing, a place where even the mind cannot take you. It is called the body mind, an awareness that you usually find around your place of *chi,* of energy and shaman balance, around your navel. The place where you become illuminated and full of curiosity for what you cannot touch but nevertheless feel, with waves of emotion coursing through you.

Optimism or pessimism? Do you realize that if you are optimistic right now, you are healthy? Optimism can change your health. It has been scientifically proved that optimism can change your cellular structure and perhaps even the action of your DNA upon your health. If you are pessimistic right now, let us just say that if I am pessimistic right now, then I have to be honest with myself about that pessimism and I have to think, "Yeah, I am feeling a bit low. I am not very optimistic about whatever situation it is that's bothering me, or even about the world." When you become pessimistic, you lower yourself into what is actually a lower frequency by lowering your ability to feel in control of your life. Pessimism means that on some level you feel helpless. You do not feel that you have control of your life or your writing or even your writer self, and no matter what you do it probably doesn't matter a whole lot—what you do or write doesn't matter. These thoughts can paralyze you. This is a feeling you need to get rid of at all costs, this feeling of helplessness and that whatever you do does not matter. First of all, it is not true. Second, it is a disaster for your health and for your whole life. It is a real good way to ruin your life.

This all leads, of course, to an issue of self-worth. Self-worth is a feeling that you have control of your life; you have passion for something or for many things, certainly for the goodness and power of the life force, the magical mystery of your life, as the Beatles used to sing, the "Magical Mystery Tour." It is magical and it is mysterious. We don't always understand the reactions that come from other people. Oftentimes we are beset with another person's lack of self-worth, and at some point if our self-worth is greater than theirs, we have to separate and let them learn about their own limitations and heal themselves. Remember, we can't fix anybody else. We can't change anybody else, but we can change ourselves. We change ourselves by knowing on some very deep level that we have all possibility as our birthright.

# Alchemy

The world is full of possibilities. Anything you want to accomplish or write is possible. That's what makes this country so magnificent. You can be desperately immersed in your sense of the poorness of reality, the poorness of the state of your being and health, and in one instant you can change that point of view by moving out of that reality into a reality of the positive, of optimism. You can change from pessimism to this new reality now, in one moment if you wish. And with optimism, you can begin to manifest and write your dream, whatever that dream may be. If you don't know what your dream is or what you want to write but you feel inside yourself that a new writer is trying to be born, then you can start building mirrors through the experiences that you are creating in your life; you can begin to build a whole new life. This whole new life will be filled with health, with spiritual and physical abundance if that is the dream that you dream.

People say to me, "I can't help it, I can't help it. My family has always been poor. I'm from the Ozarks. I'm from Harlem. I'm from East L.A. What can I do?" Well, you can change your thought patterns. You can change the way you think about the reality from which you came and where you are in this very moment. Most of us blame everything that has occurred to us on somebody else. There are very few people who take responsibility for the life that they have created. My wonderful friend Jerry Ward had dinner with me not long ago. He was a very dear friend of Carlos Castaneda and has worked with me for years and years. And he said, "You know, Lynn, I worked with Carlos for years, and with you. And I know one thing, if I don't know anything else."

I asked, "What is that?"

He said, "You are a very dangerous woman. Carlos was a very dangerous man, and I, Jerry, am a very dangerous man."

I said, "Why do you say 'dangerous'?"

And he said, "Because you are an optimist. Because you move into the world knowing anything is absolutely possible. If you have a dream, make it huge, make it big. Push the envelope and you will reach it and many things that you have never even dreamed of. The reason we are all dangerous is because we take responsibility for ourselves."

If you take responsibility for your behavior, your world and who you are, what you have manifested, then you are someone who cannot be controlled because you stand very firmly in the center of your circle of truth. So I want to talk about self-worth for the writing spirit. I want to talk about being dangerous and being responsible for who you are and what you are, not dependent but in control of your life, your writing, and your dream. Maybe the dream has been out of reach until now; you have not been able to touch it.

To reach success as a writer, I think it is important to go deep inside of your dream and your physicalness, because they are one and the same. They complement each other; they are opposite sides of the same coin. You stand in this life with a foot in the spiritual and a foot in the physical, which is also the dream that you create. Think about your stance as a writer in the world. Is your foot in the physical stuck, cumbersome? Is your foot in the spirit strong or is it almost nonexistent? Let yourself feel something about yourself that you have not felt before. If you can, imagine yourself in different environments. You are in a beautiful paradise. Let the environment fill you with its aesthetic joy. Swim with the turtles; ancient as they are, their memories are extraordinary. Let the waves of the warm ocean carry you toward the shore and back out again. Look at the mountains surrounded by clouds. Smell the flowers; go to the fish ponds. Let yourself be taken, transported into another world for a time. Allow yourself to step out of what you have always known, your rituals of life that you have had up to this very moment. Now go to the Himalayas, with the sun reflecting like diamonds off virgin snow. Allow yourself to step out of your life long enough so that a new and different thought pattern can happen to you.

I often think of astronauts who were shot out into space in a tin can. After a few days, they came back and said they had seen the face of God. Why would that happen in such a short period of time? It happened because they were taken out of their normal by-rote life long enough for an epiphany to happen, for something completely new to drop into their consciousness. So explore this idea in your mind. Meditate on different surroundings that appear surreal to your own existence. Write down five different reactions you had to these new environments. Go around the Wheel: How did this experience feel physically? Emotionally? Spiritually? Mentally? Did you have feelings of restriction, release, fear?

Alchemy was created during the Dark Ages to hide sacred formulas from those who wanted to destroy them. It is a process of transforming something common into something special, an unexplainable and mysterious transmuting, and it intertwines with symbolism. Symbolism is actually an expression of alchemy. As a writer, you become an alchemist as you take the world of the ordinary and transform it into mystery, when you take ordinary words and transform them into expressions of great beauty and wisdom and joy, when you are able to so entertain your readers that they perhaps lose all sense of time because they do not want to put your writing down.

In *Alchemy: An Introduction to the Symbolism and the Psychology*, Marie-Louise von Franz notes that the alchemy of ancient Egypt was often expressed through myth. One such myth that comes to mind is the "belly of the closed house." The closed house or closed door in ancient Egypt was represented by the coffin, that place where the king "married" his mother, as in the union of Isis and Horus or Hathor and Horus. The priest would say, "Now you stay uniting in love with your mother" as he closed the door of the funeral chamber. It is in the "belly of the closed house" that the union of opposites occurs, the integration of opposites, the integration or balance of the masculine and the feminine, and it is symbolized in the world as the peacock, which is the symbol for the renewal of life. A Zen master would say, "He has the door of his heart closed so that no one can guess his feelings."

One becomes a mystery to others because of the oneness of self. Your writing becomes an expression of your oneness with your creativity and becomes a surprise and unpredictable, not unlike a romance where the union of love becomes a movement of the spirit in search of fulfilling itself. What has been held secret in the chambers of your heart begins to beckon, and you discover your very own brand of personal power. By closing the doors to your house, resistance is created, friction and heat, the marriage of self to self, and an uncommon force begins to take hold of you. You are no longer taking part in the world. You are not wasting your energy. You are finally and at last becoming a warrior who is unpredictable and dangerous. You are writing. You have become dangerous in the sense that people can no longer predict your next move. Whether you know it or not, you have reached a crossroads of power. Now your true work begins. Alchemy, the divine transformation of lead into gold, the flame that ignites your passion, develops and burns within you.

Live as you will have wished to have lived when you are dying.
—Christian Furchtegott Gellert

# 32

## BAPTISM

Is there a baptism for newly created pieces of work? How would you divine the sacred acknowledgment of something newborn by your hand: a splash of water, a soft wind that has swept the fragrance of roses, a walk through the decorated cemetery of your ancient memories? Or would you choose a baptism that confronts your ever-present sense of death? What is the bridge, for you, between heaven and hell? To many, your choice of baptism is essential in this process. I see that as feeling worthy of your creation or taking the power that has been thrust upon you through your work. You have to grow, so often, to inherit what you've created. Sometimes that effort can take the rest of your life.

A destiny or supposed fate can be wrapped inside your words and can define your future. To live that well and to take up an efficient sword against your enemies will appear to you as fear or discrimination or even aging. You will learn to be an impeccable warrior and an ever-so-humble servant to the invisible forces that animate you. You will realize that you have been gifted, and there is no refusing that gift. Take what you find into the world and share it. Manifest your dreams and your health.

Author and teacher John Perkins talks about sitting with a friend in the winter, by a pond. The friend tossed a stone into the pond and the water turned instantly to ice.

The tossing of that stone into the water was a flash point. That's what you need as a writer, a flash point, and everything changes. The flash point for you is knowing that anything is possible and you can choose the dream you live in, because you know you are a shape-shifter. You know you are a dreamer. You know you are a writer.

If you want power, you have to make a place inside you for power to live.

Many people have asked me how they can better deal with twenty-first-century life and remain balanced in spirit. In turn, I ask them, "If you could make one act of power that would change your life forever, what do you think it would be?" This question oftentimes brings up a lot of unrest and a lot of passion, especially in women, because an act of power is an act that is performed from the deepest part of one's passion, the deepest part of one's being. It is the true manifestation of your truth into the world. An act of power is when you take all of your focus, all of your energy, all of your power and put it into one endeavor with passion.

An act of power is like a sword cutting through butter. It catapults you up. You move in a vertical South to North movement on the Sacred Wheel, taking a concept of spirit in the North; manifesting it in the South into the physical, reaping the feedback, the benefits; and then mirroring back in the North again in wisdom and strength. It is a vertical movement up through the barrier of flat energy that has been over most of our heads our entire lives. You move up above the clouds, into the golden sun-light, into a different level of vibratory rate, a different harmonic where other people who have made an act of power live. Even though you may have been shoulder to shoulder with these very same people perhaps your whole life, you probably didn't realize that their lives were so very different from yours.

When you make an act of power, you begin to manifest your true destiny in this lifetime. Your true destiny isn't just the book you write, the masterpiece of art you create, the magnificent mu-sic you compose, the family you raise. An act of power is a gath-ering of your strength, a gathering of your energy. It's a burning fire, and in the process of that fire burning away your negativity, all of your blocks and emotional baggage are burned. They are burned away. Instead of giving tremendous energy to the prob-lems that kept you from the act of power, the very fact that you made the act of power gets rid of the blocks that you had.

An act of power can only truly be made with an incredible act of will, a collection of what we call the shaman will. You chose to be born on the physical plane for a reason, to learn lessons you can learn only on the physical plane, how to deal with an act of power. When you move up into the dome of your being, to your spirit lodge, and begin to do higher spiritual work and ceremony, you must be strong physically, mentally, and emotionally. The foundation of your being must be very powerful, just as a sky-scraper cannot be built on sand. All of your baggage must be gone or the spirit lodge that you are will come tumbling down. The act of power has produced a tremendous amount of work in your life.

Through the mirrors that you have created through working, you have managed to drop all of the old baggage, the pain, diffi-culties, your childhood conditioning, and you have moved closer and closer to the center of your sacred spiral. This is your true and essential being, the home of the magnificent sacred witness, that place within yourself that is the still point. And you sit in the center, in ever-increasing stillness, knowing that you have indeed accomplished what you have come to accomplish on this earth. You have made your mark. You have changed the world in some way. You have manifested your truth and your being into the world, and now a kind of stillness inhabits your being. You begin to watch life around you, like a great wise one.

We spend most of our lifetimes in reaction to the world around us, in reaction to our conditioning, to what people do to us, for us, and with us, in company with us. When you reach that still point, that eye of the storm, you begin to be the prime mover in your own life. You begin to be like a goddess, simply watching, creating harmony and balance and a space of tenderness around you, of kindness and understanding. You become the teacher because it is now that you can see the travail, the pain—spiritually and physically—that people are living through.

Agnes Whistling Elk said to me so many years ago that we are all called and we are all chosen, but so very, very few of us have the courage to follow our dreams. You are a writer; you can't but follow your dreams if you are to be true to yourself.

# *Epilogue*

I feel humble for the depth of the creative spirit within us. When the flow is interrupted at the end of a book and I must let it go, I am filled with a secret grief for the surge of writing, agony, conflicts. Or is it because I lived through it again? Two of my muses didn't make it this year, Fritz Scholder and Hunter S. Thompson. Now whom do I perch with on a lonely peak and howl to the moon? It's a lonely abyss to cross, this life, without your muses. But there are a few others, different but true. We all live in each other's hearts, even after *duende* walks in your footsteps long enough to take your soul. Somehow the entropy, the energy released after creating something, floats with the creative spirits of the dead. But energy is never static and it comes back to you one day like bees laden with pollen to bring you messages of love and inspiration from the faraway.

This book is a gift of love to other intrepid spirits who are looking for a gateway into their own secret garden of talent. May you walk in beauty and success for all your days.

—*Lynn V. Andrews*

Eagle & Hawk with their great claws & hooded heads tear life to pieces
Vulture & Raven wait for death to soften it.
The poet cannot feed on this time of the world
Until he has torn it to pieces,
and himself also.

Robinson Jeffers, "Tear Life to Pieces,"
*The Beginning & the End and Other Poems:*
*The Last Works of Robinson Jeffers*

# *Writing Exercises*

### For Chapter 3: CLIMB YOUR TREE OF DREAMS
Imagine for a moment that you are a great tree, you are a tree of dreams. Visualize this tree in all its magnificent bloom. What kind of tree are you?

### For Chapter 4: DISCIPLESHIP
Take a few minutes as you are sitting quietly. Close your eyes, scan your body and find where writing lives inside you. Write about what you discover. How does it feel? Are there colors or sounds or images that come to you? For example, some writers find that writing resides in their shoulders. They describe this as a very powerful place, and when they close their eyes and move to this place, a tingle runs up and down their spines, their attention shifts, and they become open to inspiration. Play with this for a time. Write about your feelings and relationships. This is how you find your writer's voice.

### For Chapter 8: "I BELIEVE BECAUSE IT IS ABSURD"
You are the twenty-five-year-old daughter of a socialite in her fifties. You have a new family of your own, and you are spiritually oriented.

Your mother brings home a new fiancé from Europe, where she has been traveling. He is French, in his fifties also, and he works in a hotel as a concierge. He is not well-to-do but it is obvious they are very much in love. As the daughter, what is your reaction to your mother's new fiancé? How would you place this experience on the Wheel? Write a few pages.

Now write a few pages as the mother, and finally write a few pages as the fiancé.

## *Chapter 9:* DIVINING THE HIDDEN
Do a painting of yourself as a writer.

## *Chapter 10:* WRITER AS MAGICIAN
Write a paragraph from first attention, or your everyday awareness of life. Then go back and write the thoughts or words between the words. Now rewrite the paragraph, merging the physical world—what you write from first attention—with the world of spirit—the inspiration that resides between the words. How does your paragraph change?

## *Chapter 13:* KNOW YOUR ALLY
Read your words aloud. Know the consequences of their rhythm. Do they sound hollow? Read them again. Do you find yourself saying words that are different from what is on the written page? Which has the ring of clarity and truth to it?

## *Chapter 16:* WALKABOUT
What is your point of view? What is the history of your family, and how has it affected you? Where does your point of view place you on the Wheel? Do you approach your world from the East, the West, the North, or the South?

What is the point of view of your characters? Where does that point of view put your characters on the Wheel?

*Chapter 26:* CLAIMING THE INNER SPIRIT

Live a day as someone else and write about it at the end of the day. For example, see yourself as Ernest Hemingway or Danielle Steel, Georgia O'Keeffe or Anne Rice. Where do you feel the resistance in your body at the end of the day? Where do you feel joy and how do you express it?

*Chapter 31:* ALCHEMY

Put yourself in a new surreal environment and write down five reactions you had with this new environment. Then put them on the Wheel. For example, if you have lived in a city all your life, see yourself in the middle of the Sudan or the Kalahari, or in the middle of the Arctic wilderness.

Go to the Wheel. First see yourself in this new environment physically, in the South. How is that for you? Then move to the West. How are you feeling emotionally about this new landscape? In the North is spirit; what is your spiritual connection to this place? In the East is your mind. Mentally, is there a reason for you to be here? What can you learn and write about from this new place?

# The Shaman Dance
## of Power

Throughout this book, I have spoken of the importance of movement, the movement of ideas through you, the movement of words on paper, your movement through the stages of writing and manifesting your dream into the world. Many times I have talked about the importance my teachers placed on my own physical well-being and the importance of learning to move with intent.

I would like to share with you a very sacred form of movement that the Sisterhood of the Shields taught me and that I, in turn, teach my apprentices in my Mystery School. This is a sacred way of connecting with the universe, of connecting with the spirits of light that are around you all the time, of connecting with your environment and the very air that you breathe. It is a healing practice and my teachers and I often go out into nature and actually heal the wounded and damaged fibers of our world, especially when I am in an area where the energies are frayed and chaotic, such as a city clogged with traffic, a forest after the fires have swept through, leaving an empty parking lot where the earth is visibly suffocating.

## The Shaman Dance of Power

It is called the Shaman Dance of Power. I would urge you to begin to do this dance on a regular basis, every day if you can for your own sense of well-being and to increase your harmony with Mother Earth and your living environment. This dance is done very slowly, and it is an excellent way of entering into a movement meditation or stretching out the fibers of your body and your mind after a long day at work before you sit down to write, or when you have been writing for many long hours and seem to have come to that place where nothing moves. It is a way of connecting and reconnecting with the writing that moves within you.

This is the Shaman Dance of Power:

Stand. Center yourself over your shaman center; this is usually a place which is about two inches above or below your navel area. It is slightly different for different people.

Hold your arms straight above you. Place your palms together. Keep your spine very straight and bend your knees slightly. Take a deep breath. Center yourself all the way down through your body. You are like an antenna reaching up toward the universe. You are joining Mother Earth and Father Sky through the translation of your shaman body as you do this dance.

Close your eyes. Bring your arms down, with your palms still together, over your heart, and collect the energy of your body. Collect the energy around you until it feels right. No one can tell you what that feeling is, but you will know it.

Set your feet about a foot apart and bend your knees deeply. Feel Mother Earth under the bottoms of your feet.

Reach your hands back above your head, palms still together, feet apart, and bend your knees again, slowly and deeply. Then straighten your arms.

Bring your arms down, palms still together, and take a deep breath as you do so. Now separate your palms and reach out in front of you with your palms up and out. Do not straighten your elbows completely—keep them just slightly bent.

At this point, you begin to test the air for energy waves by moving your hands as if you are touching a cloud. Very gently you move around. Then you begin to feel a line of cold, or a line of warmth, and you follow it along with your fingers as though you are smoothing a feather.

Rub your hands together at this point. Then push your palms back up and out, into the air around you. With your eyes closed, begin, gently and quietly, to feel the energy flows.

Now your sensing body, your body mind that lives within your shaman center, takes over. Let your body become fluid. Let it move with what you feel. Sense the energy vectors, like shining luminescent wires of light. Run your fingers and hands over them, caressing them, healing them, and place your energy into them from your shaman center.

As you dance and work with these vectors, take a deep breath. Keep your fingers closed and your thumbs in, and cup your hands. Bring the energy into your pelvic area and up into your shaman center with both of your hands. You will feel your body start to tingle. For all that you give out to the energy vectors, you in turn take back, bringing that energy in and up through your body and out through the top of your head. Reach your hands above your body and back down again in a circular fashion.

With your eyes closed most of the time, you can follow the energy vectors through a forest, along the ocean, up to a mountaintop. You dance, dipping and swaying, with the forces of energy around you.

You are actually healing the energy vectors that are keeping this world of ours together. If those energy vectors get frayed, we will lose the atmosphere. We will lose our earth. So when you do the shaman dance of power, you are really doing something to heal the earth.

This is a wonderful exercise to do in the wind. When you feel a gust of wind come toward you, follow it with your fingers. You will begin to feel the energy within the wind. Then you can take that energy and transform it through your own body, and push it back out again.

When you are doing this dance out in nature, you won't be standing still. You will find an energy vector and follow it. Just take it wherever it leads you. It's really nice to do this in a wilderness place where you don't feel self-conscious, where you can really go with it. We in the Sisterhood have been working a lot with the energy vectors around Arizona, which were very frayed around the Phoenix area and now are just perfect. We go from one place to another, from time to time, and fix the energy vectors. It's very important.

Practice the Shaman Dance of Power at least once a week. If you experience a block in the energy of your body, perhaps a headache, depression, or writer's block, this is a good practice for you. If you don't feel vectors of energy, then use your imagination. Visualize one of your characters and begin to feel his or her energy. Is it corrupted in some way, or does it need love and care from you to bring it into full expression? Dance with your character and become it, and notice how you move. What does your character need to become visible in your writing?

# Bibliography

Andrews, Lynn V. *Medicine Woman*. San Francisco: Harper & Row, 1981.

———. *Spirit Woman*. New York: Jeremy P. Tarcher/Putnam, 2002. Previously published as *Flight of the Seventh Moon,* San Francisco: Harper & Row, 1984.

———. *Jaguar Woman: The Wisdom of the Butterfly Tree*. New York: Jeremy P. Tarcher/Putnam, 2002. Originally published San Francisco: Harper & Row, 1985.

———. *Windhorse Woman: A Marriage of Spirit*. New York: Warner Books, 1989.

———. *The Woman of Wyrrd: Arousal of the Inner Fire*. San Francisco: Harper & Row, 1990.

———. *The Love & Power Journal*. Carlsbad, Calif.: Hay House, 1999.

———. *Tree of Dreams*. New York: Jeremy P. Tarcher/Putnam, 2001.

Bly, Robert, ed. *Lorca & Jiménez, Selected Poems*. Boston: Beacon Press, 1997.

Crimmins, Jack. "Last Chance Range," from *Kit Fox Blues*. San Francisco: Eidolon Editions, 2006.

# Bibliography

Ellis, Normandi. *Awakening Osiris, The Egyptian Book of the Dead*. Grand Rapids: Phanes Press, 1988.

Franz, Marie-Louise von. *Alchemy: An Introduction to the Symbolism and the Psychology*. Toronto: Inner City Books, 1980.

García Lorca, Federico. *In Search of Duende*. New York: New Directions, 1998.

Jeffers, Robinson. "Tear Life to Pieces," in *The Beginning and the End and Other Poems: The Last Works of Robinson Jeffers*. New York: Random House, 1963.

Mindell, Arnold. *Dreaming While Awake*. Charlottesville, VA: Hampton Roads Publishing Company, Inc., 2000.

Rilke, Rainer Maria. *Letters to a Young Poet*. Translated and with a foreword by Stephen Mitchell. New York: Vintage Books, 1984.

Stafford, William. "Why We Need Fantasy," from *A Glass Face in the Rains*. San Francisco: Harper & Row, 1982.

# Credits and Permissions

Barnstone, Tony, and Chou Ping, trans. and eds. *The Art of Writing: Teachings of the Chinese Masters.* Boston: Shambala Publications, 1996. Copyright © Tony Barnstone. Quotations by Lu Ji, Sikong Tu, and Wei Quinzhi are reprinted with permission of Tony Barnstone and Chou Ping.

Crimmins, Jack. "Last Chance Range" from *Kit Fix Blues.* San Francisco: Eidolon Editions, 2006. Copyright © 2006 Jack Crimmins. Reprinted with the permission of Eidolon Editions.

DeLillo, Don. From an interview with Tom LeClair in *Contemporary Literature 23* (Winter, 1982). Quoted with permission of Don DeLillo and the Wallace Literary Agency.

Ellis, Normandi. *Awakening Osiris: The Egyptian Book of the Dead.* Grand Rapids, MI: Phanes Press, 1988. Quoted with permission of Normandi Ellis.

Franz, Marie-Louise von. *Alchemy: An Introduction to the Symbolism and*

# About the Author

PHOTO BY DELIA FREES

LYNN V. ANDREWS is a preeminent teacher in the fields of spirituality, personal development, and writing. The author of nineteen books, including the best-selling Medicine Woman series, she is the founder of the Lynn Andrews Center for Sacred Arts and Training, which offers a degree program, online courses, and writers' workshops. For additional information about the author, including her availability for lectures and personal consultations, see www.lynnandrews.com.

For the past twenty-five years, I have been sharing my learning and my path with others through my books, my Mystery School, and my retreats, at healing seminars and writing workshops, and through a Writers' Circle of my graduate students. It is my great joy to work with writers and all creative people, helping you to discover, inspire, and inform the wonderful talent that resides within you so that you can bring your own special vision into the world, where it is so urgently needed. I love hearing from you. Please write to me at:

Lynn V. Andrews
2934½ Beverly Glen Circle
Box 378
Los Angeles, CA 90077

If you would like information about my writing program, or to be on my mailing list, send me your name, address, and e-mail address.

In Spirit,

*Lynn V. Andrews*

Printed in the United States
by Baker & Taylor Publisher Services